How to Stop Living Paycheck to Paycheck

How to take control of your money and your financial freedom starting today

Complete Volume

By

Income Mastery

How to Stop Living Paycheck to Paycheck:

How to take control of your money and your financial freedom starting today

Volume 1

How to Stop Living Paycheck to Paycheck:

How to take control of your money and your financial freedom starting today

Volume 2

How to Stop Living Paycheck to Paycheck:

How to take control of your money and your financial freedom starting today

Volume 3

Table of Contents

How to Stop Living Paycheck to Paycheck: Volume 1

How to take control of your money and your financial freedom starting today

Volume 1

By

Income Mastery

Introduction

How do you take control of your money and your time? How can you enjoy your money and be able to save it at the same time? How can you achieve financial freedom and be the boss of your life? We'll explain different ways to achieve financial freedom and take control of your money and your time today.

Let's start by thinking about what financial freedom is for you. To be able to travel whenever you want? To be able to give up office work from nine to five. To have no debt. To live off your interest. To be able to retire at fifty without worries. We all have different answers but financial freedom can be achieved in the same way. It is very important to take control of our finances and to avoid living worried and stressed , paying debts and working overtime in order to pay our bills. We have to start with a clear idea of what we want to do and why we want this freedom, this will give us a direction and will give us a clearer idea of our budget.

Achieving financial freedom can be achieved in a number of ways, not necessarily by making more money. We should start by getting our finances in order and to saving money. . Is it possible to save your money and enjoy it at the same time? The answer is yes.

Knowing how to save and spend our money is critical to achieve financial freedom. Saving is not easy, spending is. It may seem impossible especially if you have never had control of your finances. This includes managing your credit cards, paying your debts, creating short- and long-term budgets, managing your monthly expenses, short- and long-term goals, amongst others. All this planning can intimidate us if we haven't done it before, but it's a matter of organization and a little work. Saving money and achieving financial freedom is learning to make conscious decisions, having determination, motivation and flexibility. We're not going to tell you that it's easy to take control of your money, but it's possible and every step of the way is worth it. Once you begin this process, you will realize that you are more disciplined than you think and that you will be able to achieve your goals without putting as much effort as you thought.

We will develop topics related to our management with credit cards, we will explain about the different types of expenses and how to eliminate or minimize them, We will also teach you how to create a budget in the short and long term, what it consists of, how they differentiate and we will teach you how to set goals you can achieve and how to achieve them. We will also explain how to organize your debts, what are the options to have lower interest rate. We will continue to use your credit, debit and cash cards. What is the difference between using them and why does it affect your savings? What is the impact of using both on your finances and how does it affect your personal freedom? This will impact and directly affects our savings and financial freedom.

In this volume we will teach you how to achieve financial freedom with simple but effective strategies.

Chapter I: How to prepare a real budget?

Let's start this process. The first thing we need to do before we start working on our budget is to evaluate our financial health. It is very important to know how much debt we are in, , we need to know which Banks we owe money to, , we also need to understand what is the interest rate that each debt has and what is the total amount that we need to pay. . Once we have the full amount of our debts, we need to evaluate if we can pay them in one instalment or how long it will take us to pay them fully.. This gives us an indication of how we are financially and what measures we should take. We must pay our debts in order to save most of our money.

Once we have calculated our debts, we can begin to assemble our budget which will include our income and expenses. It is very important to be honest with ourselves and add all the debts we have no matter how small. Once this is done, we have to analyze what kind of debts we have. Do they accrue interest? Is it possible to pass all our debts to a single entity? Realistically, how soon can we pay for them without putting the rope around our necks? It is very important to know how much the interest rate on our cards is and how it is calculated. Banks offer to purchase debt and place it in monthly fees with a fixed interest rate usually lower than the interest rate on our credit card. If you want to pay your debts in fixed fees and your bank offers this option at a good interest rate, you should consider the amount you must pay monthly and the amount of fixed fees which your bank allows you to accommodate them. The more you pay upfront, the less we have to pay each month. There are banks that allow us to pay our debts and fees monthly up to 3 years.

Everything will depend on the plans we have and how much we are willing to save in order to pay our debts faster which is what we recommend. Bear in mind in mind that we can also make payments to the capital of the debt without paying interest. Paying our debt in this way will help us enter the credit financial system and qualify for credit. It is very important that we pay our debts on time. This will give us a good credit score. We can also consider for another bank to buy our debt. For example, if you have debts with Bank A, Bank B will probably be able to buy the total amount with a smaller percentage of what Bank A offers. In this case, we could move the debt and put it into installments as well.

Once we have analyzed which is the best option for us, we can begin to elaborate our budget. It's easier to start with a short-term Budget which one from one to three years, and then continue to work on our long-term Budget which is from four to ten years.

Let's start by asking how much is our income? We must take into account not only our monthly income but whether we will have any additional income or not the additional income to take into consideration can be interest from our savings account, a birthday gift in cash that we receive every year, or perhaps income from renting property. We must take into account real numbers, do not add that increase that might come or some freelance work that could get offered to us. It is necessary that these numbers are realistic and true and that we take into account the amount of taxes to be paid. Once we have this number, we'll continue with the expenses.

We will start with the fundamental expenses such as the rent of our apartment or house or our mortgage, food and drinks you consume, monthly utilities (water, electricity, electricity, water, etc.), our transportation expenses and the amount we pay for our insurance. All of these expenses are essential and most are fixed. Utilities can vary from month to month depending on usage, so it's important to use the month with the most expenses and use it in our budget as our fixed monthly expense to save surprises. If the expenses are less than expected, it is important to keep that amount saved that month and use it to pay our debts that would be more convenient.

We also have to consider our intermittent expenses which will vary throughout the year such as the maintenance of our car or taxes that we must pay as vehicle tax each quarter. We should also consider if it is cheaper to pay annually s such as health insurance. Many companies offer discounts to their customers if a payment is made for a longer period of time. This alternative should be considered in order to try to minimize and reduce our expenses as much as we can.

 One way to a budget is to take into account all the expenses we have made in the previous twelve months, analyze them and divide them by twelve. This will give us an idea of how much we have spent the previous month and year, what we have spent on and how our spending fluctuates.. Seeing how much we've spent is also going to help us reconsider our spending. When we realize how much we spend on coffee daily, it will be easier for us to reconsider our habits and become more aware of the purchases we make. We recommend increasing this amount by ten or fifteen percent because it will help us to have an emergency fund for any additional unbudgeted payment such as a car repair or an emergency repair needed in our house or apartment. . It also helps us in case of any unexpected increase in any of our accounts. If we do not use this amount, instead of spending it on items that we do not need and we can consider luxury. Little by little, with a little discipline, we will begin to save more money and will be able to achieve financial freedom.

For our short term budget it is very important to take into account the fixed membership fees of our credit cards, many people do not take into account this amount although it is a considerable amount if we have more than one card. This amount will vary depending on the financial institution and the type of card we have. We should start by checking how many credit cards we have and which ones we usually use. In the case of having more than one card from the same bank which is usually the case, we recommend verifying what is the interest rate of purchases per card and consult if you can unify lines, this way, we can save the membership payment. Unifying them mean s an increase on our credit line in case of an emergency.

It is also important to know how much is the minimum monthly expense that we must generate in order not to pay for this membership. What requirements does the bank have to be exonerated from it? It is very important to evaluate it since if we have too many credit cards that do not generate benefits it is better to evaluate if it is better to cancel it. Is it really worth paying for four or five different memberships annually? Do we use all the cards? These questions will help us plan which is going to be the best strategy for managing our money and credit cards, which ones we cancel and which ones we keep.

How to make this decision? We have to ask ourselves what is the benefit that we have with each card, we have to revise what is the interest rate applied in our purchases if we cannot pay with cash or if we cannot pay the total amount of money spend to the bank. We also need to take into consideration , if the card allows us to pay in installments without interests, if it offers us some added value like discounts in purchases in stores where we buy regularly. This simple exercise will help us save money. It will reduce our expenses and help us achieve of our short- and long-term goals.. It will also change the relationship we have with credit cards, once we realize what is the additional item, we must pay for an item by paying it with credit card instead of paying it in cash, we will think about using it twice.

Now that we have our budget (we have subtracted our expenses from our actual income) and have made important decisions about our credit cards, we must ask ourselves if we have any money left, if we have a d or a surplus,. We need to be certain that we can save money and if we have a deficit we need to make sure we cut expenses..

Savings are achieved when our expenses are less than our income which allows us to save money, no matter how small. We also recommend saving for an emergency fund. This can be used in case of an emergency, we can also use this to our debts and this extra amount saved can also help us to generate more interest in our savings account which means we can obtain more income. It should not be seen as money that can be used in any situation, as the name implies, it is only for emergencies such as some treatment at the hospital related to our health. Doing this simple calculation will help us on our way to financial freedom, since we will know how much we spend monthly. This number will determine how much we can save or how much or many expenses we have to cut or reduce and which ones. We should always consider that it is possible to increase our income in different ways, not necessarily with a salary increase in our job but we can also have an additional job such as working for FreeLancer , we can , invest or switching to a type of savings account that generates more interest. This must be assessed by analyzing different Banks , their pros and cons, our time and what we really want.

Chapter II: Reducing Your Expenses

Speaking of savings, at this point, we can't help but look at our expenses. Why? Knowing what we spend on, how much we spend, how we spend and what our priorities are is going to help us on the road to financial freedom.

The most obvious answer to saving and reducing our expenses is that we have to start living below our income It sounds like an obvious answer, but it's not. We have to ask ourselves why to do we overspend? Why do we get into debt using our credit cards and paying very high interest rates? Do we really need to spend money on items which are not necessary for us_? Are these items vital to our happiness? Can we live without these expenses?

Let's start with expenses that we can cut and/or reduce and analyze our subscriptions. How many subscriptions do we have with automatic debit or debit to the credit or debit card? Are all our subscriptions really necessary? Can we find an alternative? Is it really necessary to have Spotify Premium? Is Netflix vital to our life? Are we really using that gym membership? Do we have to go to the most expensive gym?

The first month we recommend at least cutting off one subscription and the following week or the following month another one. , We recommend looking for alternatives to see where we can watch movies or series on the Internet, where we can listen to music, if we can download it in another way or what would be the cheapest alternative. This will validate our decision and make us feel that we are not losing part of our comfort. You will realize that you do not need to make these expenses and that that money is better invested in the payment of your debt or that it can be saved in order to achieve that financial freedom you want so much. Do you have to work so many hours a day to be able to pay those subscriptions? The answer is really no.

As we have already mentioned, it is really important to start making conscious decisions and to be disciplined. When we begin to see the amount of money, we have saved , we will feel more motivated. Before buying something new, it is very important to ask ourselves what the purpose of the purchase is we are going to make. Will that new pair of shoes or wallet help us obtain the increase we want? Will it help us obtain the financial freedom? Where will it be better invested? These items will not help us gain financial freedom and will be better invested in a savings account earning interest. This type of non-vital expenses can be cut and that surplus can be used to pay off our debts or can be saved. Does it really make a difference to cut and/or reduce these expenses?

Of course, adding them together, we realize that if we spend fifty dollars a month, we spend annually six hundred dollars that can be invested, in four years it will be two thousand four hundred dollars that could be used to pay the capital of our debts or saved. How long have we had these subscriptions? Let us remember that the more we save in less time, the faster we will achieve financial freedom.

We must take into account the costs of our house if we rent it. We have to analyze the price of it. Let's ask ourselves if the price is within the market, if we could live somewhere nearby with similar features for a cheaper price, if it's really worth spending so much money on this particular rental. Why would you prefer to live in a more expensive place if you could save hundreds of dollars a year for a place with the same features nearby or even on the same block? This change of mentality and the possibility of moving to a new house is going to mean big savings. Having a lower rent will mean that we can use that extra money to pay off our debts or save it so we can pay a higher down payment on a house and not have such a high interest debt. Most financial experts recommend not accepting any deal that costs more than one-third of your income. This is something we must consider, if we get a hundred dollars cheaper monthly housing per year are one thousand two hundred dollars saved that will help us get financial freedom, we will have control of our time and money.

On the other hand, we have to reconsider our costly expenses related to our habits. Do you smoke cigarettes? Do you drink a lot of alcohol? Do you do drugs? These habits can turn into costly addictions that can turn into serious health problems that would only lead us to continue spending our money. By quitting smoking you will see the difference not only in your savings but also in your body and health. We also recommend cutting back on the number of times you go out to drink alcohol per week with friends and don't use drugs. This will generate huge savings and you'll be one step closer to financial freedom.

Chapter III: Learn how to research, evaluate expenses and tips to save more money

One key to saving is to start researching everything we buy, analyzing and comparing prices. Many times, for our own convenience we go to the same supermarket or order the things we want online without doing much research and without much planning. How many times have we gone to the supermarket without a list of ingredients or what we should buy? This only generates additional purchases of what we think we are going to consume or what we feel like   at that moment. Without a list, we end up buying additional things because we don't know what we're going to cook and often end up throwing food away. Above all, how many times have you been into the supermarket feeling hungry and you end up buying items you   that you will never consume and that end up in the garbage can? Meal planning is critical to saving. When doing so, don't forget to take into account prices and expiration dates. Keep in mind that consuming any type of meat daily is going to be more expensive than consuming it four times a week and the remaining three days consuming beans and legumes.. You can do easy exchanges such as   buying the cheaper cut of meat cut of meat and you can look for cheaper protein alternatives. Not only will it be healthier for you, but it will also help you save money

We have to take into account the expiration date of the items we are buying, usually we do not review them and we are surprised that the following week has already expired. This will prevent us from throwing away items like ham, cheese, cookies, yogurt or items we usually forget we have in the refrigerator and pantry. When shopping at the supermarket, don't forget to compare prices and pay attention to the weight and price difference between brands. Many times, the brand of the same supermarket is cheaper, but that is not always the case. Let's look for brands that we trust but are cheaper. Those ten-cents do make a difference in our savings.

Coupons and discounts offered by supermarkets and those that we can find on the Internet help us save even more money. Coupons are a great way to save money when shopping in supermarkets. Most supermarkets have a loyalty program or have coupons or special offers. Find out what the discounts are in the supermarket you go to, if there are special discounts depending on the day or where you can get coupons. Some supermarkets have electronic machines that print them. We always recommend entering or following the supermarket page in social networks as they are usually posting different promotions. These small savings make a big difference monthly and annually. We also recommend comparing local supermarket prices with the wholesale supermarket and with other supermarkets or places where we can buy our groceries.

It might seem tedious to have to be comparing and looking for different places to do our shopping, but most supermarkets have prices and catalogs on the web, even some supermarkets are cheaper if we order our groceries online via delivery than going to buy local. Remember we also need to add the cost of transport. If we decide to buy in a wholesale market that usually has better prices and offers, we must find where to store a greater number of products in our home/ . Although it may seem difficult at first, buying wholesale is often beneficial because not only do we save on food, but we also spend less on transport. Instead of going shopping on a weekly basis, we can make our monthly purchases. This will also help us plan more for our meals and our monthly budget. After a few months, we will adjust to this new planning and even find more ways to save at the supermarket.

Another tip for your shopping is to use a basket and not a car, especially if you're shopping on time. Using the cart is more comfortable, but we tend to buy more because we see them empty and we do not have to load it, it has no weight. When we use the basket as we have to carry it, we tend to want fewer things and less weight therefore it is more uncomfortable. .

You should also be careful not to go to the supermarket during rush hour. Many times we see the other person's cart and we see some product that we had not seen or wanted to buy so you buy it.. We can avoid this by going to hours where there aren't as many people, going in focus and with our weekly, two-week or monthly shopping list. It's also better to go alone. If we go with family or friends, we tend to buy more. Usually because we don't pay attention, talk and the other person tends to give us recommendations and new ideas or dish suggestions for cooking, this increases our food budget unnecessarily.

With these tips we can maximize our savings on our supermarket purchases and our food. We must be disciplined so as not to fall into temptation or laziness to cook. Some tips are to cut all the vegetables in one day as soon as we buy them so that everything is ready and not having to be doing it every time we want to cook.

On a daily basis, we recommend paying attention to the small expenses we make without even realizing how much it affects our pocketbook and budget. The coffee we drink daily, that lunch sandwich, or the daily dessert we eat every day or every week means more expenses and less savings. Even that daily bottle of water or soda adds to our expenses. Sound familiar? Is this something you do? The question is, how can we generate more savings when we are away from home? If you're working in an office, can we bring our own food to work instead of going out to different restaurants for lunch every day? In case we can't take our food to work and we have to go out to eat we have to analyze which restaurant we have nearby. Are you hungry at eleven o'clock in the morning and do you eat sandwich? Bring a fruit from home or prepare something and anticipate this expense. Not only will your health improve, but you'll also start saving, and you'll have that money for yourself.

In case you have to go out for lunch, you need to do some research. Many restaurants have an executive menu that is cheaper than a la carte ordering. Many websites offer reservations at different restaurants with discounts of up to fifty percent if you book by that means. With these tips the lunch budget can be greatly reduced. These lunches must be properly budgeted for this reason it is so important to conduct prior research and anticipate these expenses. Ask yourself if we should really go out and eat in restaurants more than once or twice a week being able to cook at home and having the supplies to do so. How much do you spend on food? How much are you really spending on these sandwiches or these street food cravings? When we do the cost-benefit analysis we realize that by cutting these expenses and budgeting for outings to restaurants or cafes, we can save annually and/or pay our debts in less time. Are you going out with friends or family? Find and suggest a place where you don't have to consume so much, have a discount or have found a coupon.

Can you plan where to meet? Go to your friends' house, share the cost of food with everyone, or get together, but eat before you go out. This way, you'll avoid the temptation to order that pizza or hamburger when you're hungry. The most important thing in this case is to stick to it and respect the budget created. Are you going out to a bar with friends or colleagues? Have dinner at your home before so you don't have to order food during or after your departure. Ask for Happy Hour or After Office promotions or the drink of the day. You can share that two for one with one of your colleagues, moderate the amount of drink you order on your outings in order to achieve your financial freedom. These little tips help us generate and increase our savings and take us one step closer to financial freedom. It seems simple, but it requires motivation, willpower and determination. It's just a matter of planning and analysis.

Do you know how much you spend on transportation to and from work, home to friends or family, weekend outings, and shopping? When it comes to transport and savings, it is very important to know how much we are spending and what distances we are travelling. Can we see options such as taking public transport or the only way to get to our destination is driving? How close do we live? Can we generate any savings if we take a taxi or if we use a bicycle? Do you live close to people who work with you or go to the same destination and could they share a car or a taxi? These factors must be analyzed since it can allow us to reduce our expenses.. In case we drive, using the car not only generates stress but also increases the mileage to your car reducing its value, increases your expenses in gasoline and in maintenance and repairs. Begin by investigating what the public transport alternatives are, the prices and the route.

Can you walk or use the bicycle? Start by changing little by little, make a change and use the chosen means of transport twice a week, then three and in a short time you will get used to it. You'll have enough confidence that you'll always be able to mobilize yourself in this way to work, your social gatherings or wherever you need to go. You probably like it more than driving and you're more relaxed. The best option will always be to walk or ride a bicycle because apart from the fact that it has no cost, it has the plus that does not pollute, you can do your daily exercise, improve your health, reduce your stress and reduce your carbon footprint. Imagine how much you can save if you stop spending that hundred dollars a week, that's four hundred dollars a month and four thousand eight hundred soles a year. Did you already know how much you spend on transportation? Are you surprised?

Chapter IV: Learn to manage your credit cards

Do you understand how credit cards work_? To save we must understand how credit cards work , we must use them cautiously or only in emergencies if absolutely necessary. Do you know how much interest you have on the credit card? Do you know how it is calculated? Cards are very good for entering the banking system and applying for credit for buying a house or a car, but is it really necessary to use them when we go out or buy different items? The answer is no. We don't recommend taking your credit cards on outings with friends, when you go to the supermarket or when you go shopping with someone. The problem is, when we go out, we get excited and overspend. One more drink can't be that expensive, that polo shirt looks great on me or that pair of shoes will look great on me. For this reason, we recommend carrying cash for what we are going to use. Cash must be within our budget and we recommend taking it exactly to buy or pay what we need punctually.

When paying in cash at an establishment, we recommend keeping the change in a small bag and not spending it. This will increase as the months go by and we will have an additional fund without much effort. Banks have machines that change the simple into bills, this additional money should be credited to the account that generates interest or your savings account. Don't spend it and put it away. You'll notice how easily you spend without realizing it in a month and especially in a year.

If we have not withdrawn the cash, we recommend paying with the debit card because it is cash and does not generate a debt, not with the credit card. The day we go out to eat or want to buy something, it is better to check beforehand with which stores and companies our bank has a discount because they have several alliances with different stores. This allows us to buy that item we need but spend less.

On the other hand, if we have been using the credit card regularly, it is also good to review what kind of agreements it has and if our expenses have generated something positive, have we been accumulating points? What kind of points? How many points do we have and how and on what can we redeem them? Most credit cards have agreements with airlines and we can exchange our points for airline tickets.

In our short- or long-term budget will we have to make a trip? If the answer is yes, we may redeem these accrued miles instead of making the fare payment or paying less fare. It is important to travel in low season and not in high season so that tickets, establishments and food have a lower cost and reduce our budget. Points awarded by banks can usually not only be redeemed for miles, many times they are also used for hotel nights, shopping in supermarkets and even in different stores of clothing or items. This way, we can save on our next purchase.

To save it is necessary to plan the trips in advance, we recommend planning them at least one year in advance to have better prices on air tickets, hotels and tours if we need them. Also, for tours we can always find free tours for tourists. Planning always helps us save money.

Do you have applications on your cell phone that have your credit card number and information? We usually have our credit cards in food applications for our phone's delivery of items or taxis. We recommend removing the information from the card and switching to the cash payment option. It's easier to fall into temptation if we don't have cash and want to ask for something and the laziness wins. We lose the account and begin to accumulate debts because consumption is not always charged at the time of consumption. Changing all your payments to cash will make you think twice before placing an order and will make you respect your budget. It's also easier to track your spending if all payments are in cash. The next time we want to order food form the application we will think twice if that amount is out of our monthly budget and we will have to sacrifice something for that order. Thus, we will begin to cook and make better, more conscious decisions and think about what we are spending. Welcome to the world of savings and planned decisions.

What are you using technology for? Are you using it the best way? We recommend using technology as your ally. How? Automate all your monthly payments to be made directly from your savings account. This way, you'll save yourself the stress of having to pay online or going to different locations to make different card payments. It is also a very good tool and a way to be cautious and not pay more than the bill in interest. For example, if we go on a trip and/or forget to pay for a card, financial institutions generate and charge high interest per day that the debt has not been repaid. This expenditure, is absolutely unnecessary. For this reason, by automating our payments we can save ourselves this additional stress. We can pay our utilities in this way also we only have to affiliate our account to these entities and generate a direct collection. Of course, we have to check that we're not being overcharged.

A useful tool to save is to open a savings goals account in our bank, this can be done from the application, there is no longer a need to go to the bank and make those long queues and lose half a morning. This type of account parallels our savings account and helps us reach the goal we consider attainable in the time we determine. How does it work and why does it help us save? Because we cannot withdraw that money when we please or want to buy something that is not in our budget, we must continue to contribute and keep that money until we reach the goal set and agreed with the bank. The only way to withdraw the money is to close the account. This money would still go back into our savings account, but the idea is to keep it where we can't be tempted to use it. This is very useful for us since we can fix the monthly amount that we can contribute and is according to our budget to this account and also request the automatic debit from our savings account, in this way, we cannot have this cash that helps us save and reach the amount we have set as a goal.

We recommend logging in sporadically to see the amount we have already saved on our accounts with relatively little effort. This will help us to motivate ourselves and continue to create the habit of saving. We will also be surprised how some changes and adjustments in our habits can generate significant savings. It is important, and this is what we recommend, to have the application of our bank in the cell phone in order to periodically review the expenses we have made and what is the total amount of our debts. Seeing how our savings are decreasing and how they are increasing, motivates us to continue saving. Financial freedom is getting closer and closer.

On the other hand, continuing with technology, there are several very easy to use applications that help you to keep your expenses up to date. In these applications we can add our monthly, daily and even annual budget and add our daily expenses. It will automatically tell us how much we have left to spend daily and what our income is after these expenses. Seeing our expenses and adding them to the application will also help us make more conscious decisions and give us a clearer idea of what expenses we could still adjust or even eliminate.

Some of these applications can be linked to our bank account and even include coupons and offers to help us save a little more. Without effort and without thinking it we will be reducing, even more, our expenses therefore we will be increasing our savings.

Chapter V: Learn to Save

Are you having trouble saving alone? Saving is also like exercising, if you do it with some friends or family, you get more motivated and you feel compelled to do it, it can even increase your competitiveness and you want to win by saving. There are some applications where you can create a savings group by inviting your family and friends. Each account and goal are individual as is the contribution, but it is very good for achieving goals together and motivating each other. Would you be interested in making a bet with your friends or family that you can save more? Download this type of application and start saving today. It should be noted that we must verify that these applications do not have commissions, have a minimum balance or any type of commission per transaction which is the case in the vast majority. It is very important to be motivated and know that saving is a matter of planning and making conscious decisions. Your friends and families can help you reach your goals and not buy too much.

Do you love shopping online? Do you always get the offers of your favorite brands? Do you get discounts from more than twenty different stores? This is the case for most people. How to stop falling into temptation of getting items which are on sale? If you are registered to receive promotions on your email of several stores it is time to unsubscribe or send all these emails to SPAM. This will prevent us from falling into the temptation to buy what we don't need when it's at a discount. We need to start making rational, non-emotional purchases. You have to stop buying because we see an item that we liked at a discount that will end up saved because we don't need it and we can consider it a luxury item. Don't window shop. that you can't buy! You'll want to include them in your budget or just to get them. . Not being on the list of senders of this type of mails also removes the stress of wanting to buy something that is not planned or that we have not thought we need.

Some new item like a blender when ours still works perfectly, but the one we want has additional features we'll never use, but we think we need it. Sounds familiar? If we want to sign up and send us emails, we recommend that they are about finances, how to achieve your goals and financial tips. This will keep us motivated and educate us more in the management of our finances. Subscribe to pages you like; do you practice any sport? Are you interested in a particular topic? Start using your time in whatever you want and whatever you like.

These small tips prevent us from making small purchases that add up at the end of the month and help prevent us from falling into temptations.

Returning to the use of cards, in case you need to use the credit card and cannot pay the full amount before it generates interest, call your bank and ask them to put it in installments. Why do we do this? So, we don't pay interest and have to pay the bank more than the item alone cost us. Remember that the interest is calculated on the total amount we have not paid, that is, if your interest on purchases is fifty percent and you could not pay one hundred dollars, we will have to pay the additional half of the item purchased. Have you thought about it this way before? Imagine how much more we have paid to the banks for not paying the full amount of our debts.

This is going to be that we respect our budget for our departures and do not spend more than we should. We can also see how much we are actually spending. As we have recommended, it is very important to know how much we are spending, and to add all our expenses to some of the applications in the cell phone that we have chosen and that help us determine this amount. Knowing what we are spending on we can also cut additional costs, for example, if our daily food spending budget is twenty dollars, we can see what we are actually spending on. We'll think twice before we buy that coffee we can have at home.

Another way to save a little more without much effort is to search for coupons on the internet. There are websites that offer discounts in restaurants, hotels and restaurants. But the most important thing is to think before buying something we don't need.

To establish our short-term savings goal, we can start planning for one to three years. We should think about saving so that we can live from three to nine months to pay the daily expenses just in case, since we don't know what could happen in the future in the company where we work or in the economy of our country. We must save cash to pay for our vacations and large purchases like a car. The long-term savings plan should be four years or more and should include the startup of a home or remodeling project, the education of your children, and the retirement you so much dream of. We may also consider investing our money in an investment account which, while representing a risk, also indicates an opportunity to grow as the market grows.

Setting a smaller savings goal, such as buying a cell phone, can give us the psychological boost that makes the immediate sense of saving rewarding and a habit.

In the social sphere, do you check everything you pay? It's a very bad habit, but we don't usually check the bills we pay or verify what we sign or check the ballot. Unbelievable, isn't it? How many of us are guilty of this? We recommend that, if you're going out with friends and they ask for the bill at a bar, for example, that you verify that they haven't loaded any of their drinks into your account so that you don't overpay. Do your friends or family want to split the bill and you've only consumed one dish? Avoid doing this, explain that you are in savings mode and that you will only pay for what you have consumed. This will most likely prevent your bill from being three times more expensive than your consumption. Do you tip in restaurants? Consider downloading an application that calculates how much tip to leave and add it to your expenses.

Do you think saving is going to be boring? Do you think your social life is going to suffer or are you already stressed and missing those outings to bars and restaurants every weekend or three times a week? Do you think you won't be able to have fun because you are saving and can't go out with friends? That's not true. You can change your leisure and recreational habits for new and more affordable ones. This will help you find the perfect balance between fun and responsibility - you'll be saving, having fun and exploring at the same time! Try it and be surprised, you could have more fun and have new friends exploring these options.

Free events in your city? Yes! Stay on top of your community's free events, follow them on social networks, search for groups on Facebook or various community pages where people comment and share these types of events. Does my city have free events? Yes, all cities have an itinerary of free recreational activities for all citizens. For example, some of the free activities they do are screenings of different movies in parks, free classes in different sports, dance or aerobics, art exhibits, and community events funded by donations. Visit them and change your routine. You'll get more involved with the community, meet new people, and explore these new kinds of fun activities you wouldn't have experienced had it not been for this life change.

Lowering our recreational costs will help us save and stay within our monthly budget and may even help us save more than we have budgeted. On the other hand, if you're used to playing video games or buying games online or for the Nintendo Switch you can make a change and look for free games or just change activity or add it to our new day, we recommend you start reading. Reading is a free activity that you can do without spending money. There are pages and applications that provide complete and free books. Does your city and district have a library? There are many second-hand stores that have very cheap books. Try it and you'll see your savings account increase.

Do you know your city? Have fun exploring with your friends, doing activities like walking, without having to spend a lot of money or even anything at all. There are different cultural activities such as free museum nights, free tours of your city center and a range of activities you can do for free.

Are you worried about financial freedom in twenty years? Consider opening a retirement account. It is really important that we have this account in plans so that we can achieve financial freedom in the long term. If we want to achieve financial freedom, we need to start thinking about retiring.

When do you want to retire? On this will depend the amount of money that we will have to keep in order to retire earlier. While everyone's situation is different, experts recommend contributing at least ten percent of your monthly income to your retirement account so you can maintain your current lifestyle without worry. Does that sound like a high number? When you begin to make the small changes in your habits already mentioned you will realize that this number is attainable and that you could even contribute a little more. Another option is to check with your employer about contributing to a retirement plan. Companies have agreements and alliances with different financial centers so these accounts allow automatic deposits for a specific amount of your monthly salary. Consider that the money that is deposited into this specific account will not be subject to the same rates as the rest of your salary. Simple, isn't it?

Chapter VI: How to generate more savings

Do you want to save even more money? Then it is absolutely necessary that you start to pay attention to the amount of electricity you consume daily in our home. Do you sleep with the television on? Do you leave the lights on? Do you turn that room lamp off before going out or does it stay on all night and all morning? It may seem harmless and that consumption is not much, but these small oversights increase our monthly electricity bill accordingly annually and affect our savings goal. Using the drying machine daily or more than once a week also consumes a lot of electricity. We must take into account the time it takes to dry clothes to be able to program when and how we are going to wash our clothes in order to reduce our electricity consumption. The thermal also consumes electricity, in order to reduce it, can be turned off daily or when we go away from home for several days or holidays. These small changes will not only help to increase your savings but you will also be helping the planet.

These small changes in our daily habits have a positive impact on our finances. We have different options and simple strategies to start saving and achieve our financial freedom. Recover your time and control your money by following our advice. The first step will be to evaluate our financial health, how much do we really owe to the banks? Do we owe some other kind of entity? You have to start by being completely honest with yourself. Then we must see how we can pay this debt monthly without accumulating so much interest, we can talk to our financial institution and request a debt purchase. This means that we will have the option of paying in installments for a certain period of time at a lower interest rate. This gives us the opportunity to better organize our budget and lower the interest expense on purchases we have already made.

Therefore, we could convert our total debt into a fixed monthly installment for a certain number of times according to our goal and within our payment possibilities. We may also ask another financial institution to buy our debt and compare which one has the best interest rate for us. The type of payment would be the same. Once we have the exact amount of our debt, we must calculate how much money we actually have in the month, after we have paid our fixed and basic expenses. This will give us an idea at the beginning of what changes we need to make in order to start saving and how many expenses we need to reduce or cut.

Starting with simple actions like budgeting our expenses, using saving vouchers, amongst other actions. You need to know your monthly income and become aware of how much we spend and on what. By being aware and conscious of our expenses we can get out of our debts, save and find financial freedom. These small actions throughout the months and the year will lead us to gain financial freedom and regain control over our finances and our time. Some simple actions we can perform are to keep track of what we have spent after making each purchase daily, storing the vouchers and/or recording it in the application we have chosen for the cell phone that will carry our finances. With this exercise, we will realize the type of expenses we are making and which we can cut or decrease. We'll think twice before we buy that sandwich, coffee or pair of shoes that aren't within our budget and we don't need.

CONCLUSION

Subscriptions to different programs and/or applications make our monthly and annual expenses higher, especially if we have a program or application that can replace it. This is true for example in subscriptions such as Netflix or having a Spotify Premium account. We know that we can still listen to music and watch series on other websites or applications for free and that they are not exclusive and are not the only ones. On the other hand, analyzing our fixed costs will be very helpful in evaluating the changes we can make. Is our apartment or house rent too expensive? Can we find another place with the same characteristics for less money? How much can we reduce our consumption of water and electricity? By taking shorter showers, leaving the lights and television off as well as reducing the number of times we use the clothes dryer each month, we can reduce our electricity and water bills. Turn off the water heater when you go on a trip and disconnect your electronic devices, you will be surprised by the difference in your electricity and water bill.

Going to the supermarket without a list and thinking about buying whatever you choose with your finger, with your list in mind, as you walk down the aisles? Keep a list of the food and beverages that you must buy so that you don't buy more than the bill and that in the end you have food left. By planning our week menu or even if we can of the month, we can considerably reduce our expenses. By analyzing and reviewing competitor's prices, we can also choose to buy in the cheapest place and with the best offers. Reviewing the offers, discounts and coupons offered by different supermarkets and stores will help us get a better idea of where to buy.

In addition, there are several applications that offer coupons and discounts in different supermarkets and stores. How much do you spend on transportation to and from the supermarket? Buy at a wholesaler, you could make your purchases up to once a month this will lower the cost of your food, help you plan better, spend less on transportation and help reduce the emission of carbon dioxide and thus global warming.

Log in and look for coupons and discounts, so you can start spending less. Make better decisions when planning your social and family events. Don't forget that you must also budget all outings with friends, family and colleagues. Do you want to stay within your budget? Look for restaurants with discounts on different websites, applications or check if you have any type of discount on our debit card due to the financial institution with which we are affiliated. Did you go out with friends? It is necessary to keep track of what we are consuming and pay attention to our accounts. How many times do we actually review what we are being charged and what we are paying in cash or what we are getting back in a box? It is extremely important to review our accounts, ballots and/or invoices, what we are paying and our return.

In case you are in a group and want to divide the bill if you are the person who has consumed less it would be good to explain that you are saving and that you will only pay what you have consumed. It is very important that your fast food or taxi applications do not have your credit card registered to avoid consumptions and think that you will pay them later. Let's not let laziness beat us. Pay and change the payment method in all your applications to cash. This will force us to think and be aware of what we are spending on.

We must emphasize that we must stop using our credit cards in order to save on our daily purchases. This is due to the fact that the interest generated by the card if the total amount is not paid is very high, we can even pay double what we have bought or our debt. It's easier to keep our budget and respect it if we have the right cash for our payments, if we start using the credit card we can easily get out of our budget and spend more than we can or need.

How do we get around the city daily? This also influences our budget and our savings goal. It's one of those expenses that we can reduce by researching the best way to get to work, family gatherings, the supermarket, or our friends' house. Are you going by car? Do you know what expenses are involved? When riding in our own vehicle we spend on gasoline, maintenance and pollute the environment. Apart from that, we increase the mileage of the car, which reduces its market value. What do you do? Do you have a colleague who also drives a car and wants to share the costs? Better yet, can you get to the office by public transport? It is very important to compare prices to see how much the monthly and annual savings would be. If we work close to the office we may consider walking or cycling. These would be the best options since they are free, help with daily stress, you will be exercising before and after the office and will not pollute or affect the ozone layer.

To save money we can also look for other types of organized community activities such as outdoor cinema in parks, historical walks in our city or outdoor activities. Get involved in your community, have new experiences and enjoy more by paying less and saving less. We recommend that you keep all the returns we have when paying in cash at any establishment. A good idea would be to put it in a piggy bank. Monthly or quarterly we can go to the bank to exchange often for notes and deposit it in our savings account.

Use technology to your advantage. Talk to your bank and request automatic debit in the payment of your bills this will avoid the stress of going to the financial institution to pay monthly and carelessness if we go on a trip. Every day that passes that we do not pay a debt this sum interest. Are you not very convinced of how you can use the technology in your favor? Open an account from your bank's application with a savings goal of money you cannot use and request that this money be debited directly from your account. You'll be surprised how much we spend that seems so little. Challenge your family and friends to save, download an application and create a group to invite them to save with you, each goal and each deposit will be individual, but they will motivate each other. Download the application that carries your expenses, check them periodically, think that expenses such as coffees and dinners can reduce. Motivate and check periodically what is the amount you are already saving, check that all payments with automatic debit have been made and relax. Send SPAM or request that you no longer get discounted emails from your favorite stores, do you really need that new pair of shoes? Do you need that new working blender that you'll never understand or use? Not really.

All of these suggested changes will not only change our routine, they will also change your mentality and your relationship and understanding of finances and money. It will help you save in an easier way than the one you expected, we will be able to reach our goals and achieve financial freedom, we will learn and regain control of our money and time. These small changes in our daily routine will help us reach our financial goals, pay our debts and have our emergency fund. We shouldn't be stressed about money; we should have better handling. We don't necessarily need that increase or additional work, we must learn to reduce and minimize the additional luxury expenses we have and we must learn to make rational, conscious, planned and unemotional decisions. Start today and change your life! Save today!

How to Stop Living Paycheck to Paycheck: Volume 2

How to take control of your money and your financial freedom starting today

By

Income Mastery

Chapter 1: What is financial freedom?

This is the moment when you do not depend on external income to maintain your standard of living, thanks to the fact that your passive income is sufficient to cover your expenses. Therefore, you no longer need a job to live.

Passive income is money that a person earns without depending on how much time is invested.

For example:

- Interest and earnings on your investments.

- Rental of real estate or parking.

- Income earned through a website, etc.

It is necessary to know the different levels of financial freedom that exist:

- Financial security: When an individual has passive income that covers his or her living expenses (water, electricity, rent, food, basic needs, etc.).

- Financial independence: Refers to when an individual has enough money to cover his or her living expenses.

- Absolute Independence: Is when an individual has enough or many more passive incomes than he or she could spend with his or her lifestyle.

What is the difference between financial freedom and financial independence?

Most people will tell you they mean the same thing. They'll say it's just a difference in terminology that can be used interchangeably.

What is financial freedom?

Debt Free: Absolutely Debt Free. The money that a financially free person makes goes to no one but them (and unfortunately through taxes, to the government).

Emergency Savings: Have a level of savings (available immediately) that will sustain you during any period of loss of income or cover unexpected expenses. The general rule is 6 months of spending, but your goal should depend on your comfort level, income stability and earnings.

Retirement Savings: Enough money saved (invested) to cover social security or a pension at retirement so anyone can live comfortably without changing their typical lifestyle. Again, a general rule for retirement savings is to eliminate 15% of your gross income while working, preferably in tax-protected accounts.

Insurance: May not apply to everyone, but there are a number of insurance options available. Home, car, life, health, etc. The point is that you must have enough insurance to protect yourself from catastrophic loss.

Long-term care: Everyone ages. It's an inevitable fact of life that I wish wasn't true. That said, get ready for the most expensive part of your life. Health care, while a worthwhile expense, could leave you without money. If you are not ready to face the challenges of the future, you will have limited options. Think about your preferences for home care, nursing homes, and rehabilitation centers. If you rely on your children to take care of you financially, keep in mind that it will severely affect your chances of financial freedom.

What is financial independence?

"Financial independence is the financial status of an individual or family that meets the requirements of financial freedom with a couple of variations. The ultimate goal for a person or family who strives to be financially independent is to have the option of retiring earlier or continuing to work (on their own terms).

Covered debt: If used with care, covered debt can be used to finance investments that can help create wealth. This means that you are using debt as leverage to finance an investment that is secured by an asset. A common example of covered debt is a mortgage on a rental property. The mortgage is the debt. Property is the asset that "covers" the debt. In other words, if the property were sold, you would pay the mortgage in full. Covered debt is not necessary to meet the conditions of financial independence but is often used to obtain it.

Retirement savings: Strive to save enough for the traditional retirement period so you don't have to rely on supplementary social security income or a pension. Income from social security or a pension is just the icing on the cake. Maximizing tax-advantaged accounts may or may not be the best strategy for everyone, but generally it is. Savers who maximize their accounts with tax advantages generally do so to defer/avoid taxes or for succession/heritage purposes.

Investment Income: Those seeking to be financially independent generally have a significant portion of their investments in taxable accounts. One technique is to have enough savings in taxable accounts to accommodate a retirement rate that will last until the period in which you can begin withdrawing your retirement savings. Then withdrawals would begin from retirement accounts to the end of life. Another strategy is to have enough in taxable accounts where investment income would cover all expenses for life (including travel and fun things), thus allowing minimal withdrawals from tax-advantaged accounts later in life. Basically, cash flow from investments replaces earned income, freeing you from relying on others for a living.

What's the difference?

There's not much difference. Financial freedom means you have no debts and are financially stable. You are prepared to deal with what life throws at you without the worry of living from one paycheck to another. You're working, enjoying life and preparing for a comfortable retirement.

On the other hand, financial independence takes you to another level. You're the epitome of living below your means. You're saving all you can and you're investing or running your own business. You'll retire early, do whatever you want, and you'll have to explain yourself to no one.

Chapter 2: **Steps to follow to achieve financial freedom:**

Achieving financial freedom is a goal for many people. It usually means having enough savings, investments and cash on hand to afford the lifestyle we want for ourselves and our families and a growing savings that will allow us to retire or pursue the career we want without being driven by earning a certain amount each year. Too many of us fail to achieve that goal. We are overwhelmed by increased debt, financial emergencies, wasteful spending, and other problems that keep us from reaching our goals. It happens to everyone, but these twelve habits can put you on the right path.

1. Set life goals

A general desire for "financial freedom" is too vague a goal. What does it mean to you? Write down how much you should have in your bank account, what lifestyle involves, and at what age it should be achieved. The more specific your goals are, the more likely you are to achieve them. Then count back to your current age and set financial milestones at regular intervals. Write it all down carefully and place the goal sheet at the beginning of your financial folder.

2. Make a budget

Making a monthly family budget and sticking to it is the best way to ensure that all bills are paid, and that savings are on the way. It is also a monthly routine that reinforces your goals and reinforces your resolve against the temptation to squander.

3. Pay credit cards in full

Credit cards and similar high-interest consumer loans are toxic to wealth creation. Proposes to pay the total balance each month. Student loans, mortgages and similar loans generally have much lower interest rates, making it less of an emergency to repay.

4. Create automatic savings

Pay yourself first. Enroll in your employer's retirement plan and make full use of any matching contribution benefits. It is also advisable to have an automatic withdrawal for an emergency fund that can be used for unexpected expenses and an automatic contribution to a brokerage or similar account. Ideally, the money should be withdrawn the same day you receive your paycheck, so it never touches your hands, avoiding temptation altogether. However, bear in mind that the amount recommended for savings is much debated; and in some cases, the viability of such a fund is also in doubt.

5. Start investing now, if you haven't already done so

There is no better or proven and true way to grow your money than through investment. The magic of compound interest will help your money grow exponentially over time, but it takes a long time to achieve significant growth. Don't try to be a stock picker or trick yourself into thinking you can be the next Warren Buffett. There can only be one. Open an online brokerage account that allows you to learn how to invest, create a manageable portfolio, and automatically make weekly or monthly contributions.

6. Take care of your credit line

A person's credit score determines what rate is offered when buying a new car or refinancing a home. It also affects seemingly unrelated things, such as automobile insurance and life insurance premiums. The reasoning is that a person with reckless financial habits is also reckless in other aspects of life, such as driving and drinking. That's why it's important to get a credit report at regular intervals to make sure there are no erroneous black marks to ruin your good name.

7. Negotiate

Many people are hesitant to trade in goods and services and worry that it will make them look cheap. Overcome this cultural disadvantage and you could save thousands each year. Small businesses, in particular, tend to be open to negotiation, where buying in bulk or repeating business can open the door to good discounts.

8. Continuing Education

Review all applicable changes in tax laws each year to ensure that all adjustments and deductions are maximized. Stay up to date with financial news and stock market developments, and don't hesitate to adjust your investment portfolio accordingly. Knowledge is also the best defense against those who take advantage of unsophisticated investors to make quick money.

9. Adequate maintenance

Taking good care of the property makes everything from cars and lawnmowers to shoes and clothes last longer. Since the cost of maintenance is a fraction of the replacement cost, it is an investment that should not be lost.

10. Live by your own means

Mastering a frugal lifestyle with a mentality of living life to the fullest with less is not so difficult. In fact, many wealthy individuals developed the habit of living below their means before reaching wealth. Now, this is not a challenge to adopt a minimalist lifestyle or a call to action to head into the trash can with the things you've accumulated over the years. Just making small adjustments by distinguishing between the things you need rather than those you want is a financially useful and healthy habit to put into practice.

11. Get a Financial Advisor

Once you've reached a point where you can discern whether you've accumulated a decent amount of wealth, whether it's liquid investments or assets that are tangible but aren't readily available for cash conversion, a counselor is strongly recommended to educate you and help you make decisions.

12. Take care of your health

The principle of proper maintenance also applies to the body. Some companies have limited sick days, so it's a noticeable loss of income once those days run out. Obesity and ailments cause insurance premiums to skyrocket, and poor health can force early retirement with lower monthly incomes.

These steps won't solve all your money problems, but they will help you develop useful habits that can lead you to financial freedom.

Chapter 3: What are financial statements?

Financial statements are written records of a company's financial position. They include standard reports such as the balance sheet, profit and loss statements, and cash flow statement. They are highlighted as one of the most essential components of business information, and as the primary method for communicating financial information about an entity to third parties. In a technical sense, financial statements are the sum of an entity's assets and liabilities at a given time. In general, financial statements are designed to meet the needs of many users, particularly current and potential owners and creditors. Financial statements are the result of simplifying, condensing and aggregating various data obtained mainly from the accounting system of a company (or an individual).

Aims and Objectives

"The objective of financial statements is to provide information about a company's financial photo, performance and changes in their assets and liabilities that is useful to a wide range of users in making economic decisions. Financial statements must be understandable, relevant, reliable and comparable. The assets, liabilities, equity, income and expenses reported are directly related to an organization's financial situation.

The financial statements are intended to be understood by readers who have "a reasonable knowledge of economic, commercial and accounting activities and who are willing to study the information diligently. Users can use financial statements for different purposes:

Owners and managers require financial statements to make important business decisions that affect their continuing operations. A financial analysis of these statements is then conducted to provide management with a more detailed understanding of the figures. These statements are also used as part of the management's annual report to shareholders.

Employees also need these reports to make collective bargaining agreements (CBAs) with management, in the case of unions or for people discussing their compensation, promotion and classification.

Potential investors use financial statements to assess the viability of investing in a business. Investors often use financial analyses and prepare them by professionals (financial analysts), which provides them with the basis for making investment decisions.

Financial institutions (banks and other lending companies) use them to decide whether to provide a new working capital company or extend debt securities (such as a long-term bank loan or bonds) to finance expansion and other significant expenses.

Rules and Regulations

Different countries have developed their own accounting principles over time, making international comparisons of companies difficult. To ensure uniformity and comparability between financial statements prepared by different companies, a set of guidelines and rules is used. Commonly referred to as Generally Accepted Accounting Principles (GAAP), this set of guidelines provides the basis for the preparation of financial statements, although many companies voluntarily disclose information beyond the scope of those requirements.

Recently there has been a push towards standardization of accounting rules made by the International Accounting Standards Board ("IASB"). IASB develops International Financial Reporting Standards that have been adopted by Australia, Canada and the European Union (only for listed companies), are being considered in South Africa and other countries. The U.S. Financial Accounting Standards Board is committed to converging U.S. GAAP and IFRS over time.

Audit and legal implications

Although laws differ from country to country, an audit of the financial statements of a public company is generally required for investment, financing and tax purposes. These are generally performed by independent accountants or audit firms. The results of the audit are summarized in an audit report that provides an unqualified opinion on the financial statements or ratings as to their fairness and accuracy. The audit opinion on the financial statements is generally included in the annual report.

There's been a lot of legal debate about who an auditor is responsible for. Since audit reports tend to be addressed to current shareholders, it is commonly thought that they have a legal duty to care for them. But this may not be the case as determined by customary law precedent. In Canada, auditors are liable only to investors who use a prospectus to buy shares in the primary market. In the UK, they have been held accountable to potential investors when the auditor knew the potential investor and how they would use the information in the financial statements. Today, auditors tend to include in their report the responsibility to restrict language, discouraging no one other than the addressees of their report from trusting it. Liability is an important issue: in the UK, for example, auditors have unlimited liability.

In the United States, especially in the post-Enron era, there has been substantial concern about the accuracy of financial statements. Corporate officers, the chief executive officer (CEO) and the chief financial officer (CFO), are personally responsible for fair financial reporting that provides an accurate sense of the organization to those who read the report.

Financial Reports

According to the Financial Accounting Standards Board, financial information includes not only financial statements, but also other means of communicating financial information about a company to its external users. The financial statements provide useful information for investment and credit decisions and for evaluating cash flow prospects. They provide information about a company's resources, claims to those resources, and changes in resources.

Financial information is a broad concept that encompasses financial statements, notes to financial statements, supplemental information (such as price changes) and other means of financial information (such as management discussions and analyses, and letters to shareholders). Financial information is nothing more than a source of information needed by those who make economic decisions about business enterprises.

"The main focus of financial information is information about earnings and their components. Profit information based on accrual accounting generally provides a better indication of a company's current and continuing ability to generate positive cash flows than the one provided by cash receipts and payments."

Limitations on Financial Statements

The limitations of financial statements are those factors that a user must take into account before relying on them excessively. Knowledge of these factors could result in a reduction of the funds invested in a business, or actions taken to investigate further. The following are all limitations of the financial statements:

Dependence on historical costs. Transactions are initially recorded at cost. This is a concern when reviewing the balance sheet, where the values of assets and liabilities may change over time. Some items, such as marketable securities, are modified to match changes in their market values, but other items, such as fixed assets, do not change.

Therefore, the balance sheet can be misleading if a large part of the amount presented is based on historical costs.

Inflationary effects. If the inflation rate is relatively high, the amounts associated with assets and liabilities on the balance sheet will appear excessively low, as they are not being adjusted for inflation. This applies primarily to long-term assets.

Unrecorded intangible assets. Many intangible assets are not recorded as assets. Instead, any expense incurred to create an intangible asset is immediately expensed. This policy can drastically underestimate the value of a business, especially one that has spent a great deal to build a brand image or develop new products. This is a particular problem for start-ups that have created intellectual property but have so far generated minimal sales.

Based on a specific time period. A financial statement user can get an incorrect view of a company's financial results or cash flows by looking at just one reporting period. Any period may vary from a company's normal operating results, perhaps due to a sudden increase in sales or seasonal effects. It is best to view a large number of consecutive financial statements to get a better view of ongoing results.

It is not always comparable between companies. If a user wants to compare the results of different companies, their financial statements are not always comparable, because entities use different accounting practices. These problems can be located by examining the disclosures that accompany the financial statements.

Subject to fraud. A company's management team may deliberately skew the results presented. This situation can arise when there is undue pressure to report excellent results, such as when a bonus plan requires payments only if the reported sales level increases. One might suspect the presence of this problem when reported results reach a level that exceeds the industry standard.

There is no discussion of non-financial matters. Financial statements do not address non-financial issues, such as the environmental care of a company's operations or how well it works with the local community. A company that reports excellent financial results could be a failure in these other areas.

Not verified. If the financial statements have not been audited, this means that no one has examined the issuer's accounting policies, practices and controls to ensure that it has created accurate financial statements. An audit opinion accompanying the financial statements is evidence of such a review.

No predictive value. Information in a set of financial statements provides information about a company's historical results or financial status at a specific date. Statements do not necessarily provide any value for predicting what will happen in the future. For example, a company might report excellent results in one month and no sales in the following month, because a contract it trusted has ended.

Financial statements are often quite useful documents, but it's worth knowing about past problems before relying too much on them.

Chapter 4: Principles of Financial Statements

A company's basic financial statements include 1) balance sheet (or statement of assets and liabilities), 2) income statement, 3) cash flow statement, and 4) statement of changes in owners' equity or stockholders' equity. Lists the assets, liabilities of the entity and, in the case of a corporation, the stockholders' equity at a specified date. The income statement presents a summary of an entity's net income, gains, expenses, losses and net income or loss for a specified period. This statement is similar to a moving picture of the entity's operations during this time period. The statement of cash flows summarizes an entity's cash receipts and cash payments related to its operating, investing and financing activities during a particular period. A statement of changes in owners' equity or shareholders' equity reconciles the beginning of the period of an enterprise's equity with its ending balance.

Items currently reported in the financial statements are measured by different attributes (e.g., historical cost, current cost, current market value, reliable net value and present value of future cash flows). Historical cost is the traditional means of presenting assets and liabilities.

The notes to the financial statements are informative disclosures attached at the end of the financial statements. They provide important information on matters such as depreciation and inventory methods used, details of long-term debt, pensions, leases, income taxes, contingent liabilities, consolidation methods and other matters. The notes are considered an integral part of the financial statements. Schedules and disclosures in parentheses are also used to present information not provided elsewhere in the financial statements.

Each financial statement has a heading, which provides the name of the entity, the name of the state, and the date or time the state covers. The information provided in the financial statements is primarily of a financial nature and is expressed in units of money. The information relates to an individual trading company. Information is often the product of approximations and estimates, rather than accurate measurements. Financial statements generally reflect the financial effects of transactions and events that have already occurred (i.e. historical).

Financial statements that present financial data for two or more periods are called comparative statements. Comparative financial statements generally give similar reports for the current period and for one or more prior periods. They provide analysts with important information about trends and relationships for two or more years. Comparative statements are considerably more significant than one-year statements. They emphasize the fact that financial statements for a single accounting period are only part of the company's continuing history.

Interim financial statements are reports for periods of less than one year. The purpose of interim financial statements is to improve the timeliness of accounting information. Some companies issue complete financial statements, while others issue summaries. Each interim period should be considered primarily as an integral part of an annual period and should generally continue to use the generally accepted accounting principles (GAAP) that were used in the preparation of the company's last annual report. Financial statements are often audited by independent accountants in order to increase user confidence in their reliability.

Each financial statement is prepared on the basis of several accounting assumptions: that all transactions can be expressed or measured in dollars; that the company will continue in business indefinitely; and that statements will be prepared at regular intervals. These assumptions provide the basis for the structure of financial accounting theory and practice and explain why financial information is presented in a particular way.

Financial statements should also be prepared in accordance with generally accepted accounting principles and should include an explanation of the company's accounting policies and procedures. Standard accounting principles require the recognition of assets and liabilities at cost; the recognition of revenues when a transaction is made and when it has been carried out (generally at the point of sale); and the recognition of expenses in accordance with the principle of correspondence (costs to revenues). Standard accounting principles further require that the uncertainties and risks associated with a company be reflected in its accounting reports and that, in general, anything of interest to an informed investor should be disclosed in full in the financial statements.

These are the 4 basic principles of financial statements:

1. Income statement

A financial report that shows an entity's financial results over a specified period of time. The time period covered is usually a month, quarter or year, although partial periods may also be used. This is the most used financial statement. The general classifications of information noted in the income statement are as follows:

- Revenue: Revenue is an increase in assets or a decrease in liabilities caused by the provision of services or products to customers. It is a quantification of the gross activity generated by a business. On an accrual basis of accounting, revenues are generally recognized when goods or services are shipped to the customer. Under the cash basis of accounting, revenues are generally recognized when cash is received from the customer after receiving goods or services. Therefore, revenue recognition is delayed on a cash basis compared to an accrual basis of accounting.

The Securities and Exchange Commission imposes stricter rules on public companies as to when revenues can be recognized, so revenues can be delayed when customer collections are uncertain.

There are several deductions that can be made from revenue, such as sales returns and sales allocations, which can be used to arrive at net sales figures. Sales taxes are not included in the income because the seller collects them on behalf of the government. In contrast, sales taxes are recorded as a liability.

Income is listed at the top of the income statement. A variety of expenses related to the cost of goods sold and selling, general and administrative expenses are subtracted from income to arrive at the net profit of a business.

There were many rules governing revenue recognition, which have been consolidated into

GAAP in connection with contracts with customers.

- Cost of Goods Sold: The cost of goods sold is the cumulative total of all costs used to create a product or service that has been sold. These costs are included in the general subcategories of direct labor, materials, and overhead. In a service business, the cost of goods sold is considered labor, payroll taxes, and the profits of those who generate billable hours (although the term can be changed to "cost of services"). In a retail or wholesale business, the cost of goods sold is likely to be merchandise purchased from a manufacturer.

In the income statement presentation, the cost of goods sold is subtracted from net sales to arrive at the gross margin of a business.

In a periodic inventory system, the cost of goods sold is calculated as beginning inventory + purchases - ending inventory. It is assumed that the result, which represents the costs no longer found in the warehouse, must be related to the goods that were sold. In reality, this cost derivation also includes inventory that was discarded, or declared obsolete and removed from inventory, or inventory that was stolen. Therefore, the calculation tends to allocate too much expense to the goods that were sold, and that were actually costs that are more related to the current period.

In a perpetual inventory system, the cost of goods sold is continuously compiled over time as the goods are sold to customers. This approach involves recording a large number of separate transactions, such as sales, scrap metal, obsolescence, etc. If cyclic counting is used to maintain high levels of recording accuracy, this approach tends to produce a greater degree of accuracy than the calculation of the cost of goods sold under the periodic inventory system.

The cost of goods sold may also be affected by the type of costing methodology used to derive the cost of the closing inventory. Consider the impact of the following two inventory costing methods:

First in, first out. Under this method, known as FIFO, it is assumed that the first unit added to inventory is the first unit used. Therefore, in an inflationary environment where prices are rising, this tends to result in lower-cost goods being charged at the cost of goods sold.

Last in, first out. Under this method, known as LIFO, it is assumed that the last unit added to the inventory is the first unit used. Therefore, in an inflationary environment where prices are rising, this tends to result in higher-cost goods being charged at the cost of goods sold.

- Gross margin (income - cost of goods sold): Gross margin is the net sale of a business less the cost of goods sold. Gross margin reveals the amount a company earns from the sale of its products and services, before deducting selling and administrative expenses. The figure can vary dramatically by industry. For example, a company that sells electronic downloads through a website may have an extremely high gross margin, since it does not sell any physical product that can be assigned a cost. Conversely, the sale of a physical product, such as a car, will result in a much lower gross margin.

  The amount of gross margin earned by a company dictates the level of funding remaining to pay for administrative and selling activities and financing costs, as well as to generate profits. It is a key concern in deriving a budget, as it drives the amount of expense that can be incurred in these additional expense classifications.

- Selling, general and administrative expenses: Selling, general and administrative (SG&A) expenses consist of all operating expenses of a company that are not included in the cost of goods sold. Management must maintain strict control over these costs, as they increase the break-even point of a business. Selling, general and administrative expenses appear in the income statement below the cost of goods sold. It can be divided into a number of expenditure items or consolidated into a single item (which is more common when the condensed income statement is presented).

The following departments and their expenses are considered within the SG&A classification:

- ❖ Accounting and legal expenses.

- ❖ Corporate expenses.

- ❖ Installation costs.

- ❖ Sales and marketing expenses.

The classification generally does not include expenses incurred by the research and development department. In addition, it does not include financing costs, such as interest income and interest expense, as these are not considered operating costs.

Selling, general and administrative expenses consist primarily of costs that are considered part of the company's general expenses, as they cannot be traced back to the sale of specific products. However, some of these costs can be considered direct costs. For example, sales commissions are directly related to product sales and yet can be considered part of general and administrative expenses. When a cost of general and administrative expenses is considered a direct cost, it is acceptable to change the cost to the classification of the cost of goods sold in the income statement.

- Operating income (gross margin - sales, general and administrative expenses): Operating income is an entity's net income, not including the impact of any financial activity or taxes. The measure discloses an entity's ability to generate revenue from its operating activities. Operating income is positioned as a subtotal in a multi-step income statement after all general and administrative expenses, and before interest income and interest expense.

The operating income formula is:

Net Sales - Cost of Goods Sold - Operating Expenses = Operating Income

You can further modify the measure to exclude non-recurring events, such as a payment associated with a lost claim. Doing so presents a better view of a company's core profitability. However, this concept can be taken too far, as incurring occasional non-recurring expenses is a normal part of being in business.

Operating income is closely monitored by investors, who want to understand the ability of a company's core operations to grow organically and make profits, without external financing and other problems that interfere with reported results. The measure can be particularly revealing when viewed on a trend line, and especially as a percentage of net sales, to see spikes and falls in the number over time. Operating income can also be compared with that of other companies in the same industry to gain an understanding of relative performance.

Business managers can fraudulently alter the operating income figure with a variety of accounting tricks, such as a different revenue recognition policy, accelerated or delayed expense recognition, and/or changes in reserves.

- Tax expense income: Income tax expense is the amount of expense that a business recognizes in an accounting period for the government tax related to its taxable income. The amount of income tax expense recognized is unlikely to exactly match the standard percentage of income tax applied to business income, since there are a number of differences between the amount of reportable income under GAAP or IFRS and the amount of reportable income allowed under the applicable government tax code. For example, many companies use straight-line depreciation to calculate the depreciation reported in their financial statements but use accelerated depreciation to obtain their taxable income. The result is a lower taxable income figure than the declared income figure. Some corporations strive so hard to delay or avoid taxes that their income tax expense is nearly zero, despite reporting large profits.

Calculating income tax expense can be so complicated that this task is outsourced to a tax expert. If so, a company generally records an approximate monthly tax expense based on a historical percentage, which the tax expert adjusts quarterly or more.

Income tax expense is reported as an item in the corporate income statement, while any unpaid income tax liability is reported in the income tax item on the balance sheet.

- Net Income or Net Loss: Net income is the excess of income over expenses. This measurement is one of the key indicators of the company's profitability, along with gross margin and pre-tax revenues. A common calculation for net income is:

Net Sales - Cost of Goods Sold - Administrative Expenses - Income Tax Expense = Net Income

For example, income of $1,000,000 and expenses of $900,000 produce a net income of $100,000. In this example, if the amount of expenses had been greater than income, the result would have been called net loss, rather than net income.

Net income is commonly used as a measure of company performance. However, it can produce misleading results in the following circumstances:

- o Cash flows (a better indicator of the company's health) may differ significantly from net profit, due to the inclusion of non-monetary income and expenses in the compilation of the net profit figure.

- o The net income derived from the cash accounting basis can vary substantially from the net income derived from the accrual accounting basis, since the former method is based on cash transactions, and the latter method records transactions independently of changes in cash flows.

o Fraudulent or aggressive accounting practices can generate unusually large net revenues that do not adequately reflect the underlying profitability of a business.

o An inaccurate focus on net income can mask other problems in a business, such as excessive use of working capital, declining cash balances, obsolete inventory, intensive use of debt, etc.

2. Balance sheet

The balance sheet is a report that summarizes all the assets, liabilities and equity of an entity at any given time. It is usually used by lenders, investors and creditors to estimate the liquidity of a business. The balance sheet is one of the documents included in the financial statements of an entity. From the financial statements, the balance sheet is presented at the end of the reporting period, while the income statement and cash flow statement cover the entire reporting period.

The typical order lines included in the balance sheet (by general category) are:

- ✓ Assets: cash, marketable securities, prepaid expenses, accounts receivable, inventory and fixed assets.

- ✓ Liabilities: accounts payable, accrued liabilities, customer prepayments, taxes payable, short-term debt and long-term debt.

- ✓ Stockholders' equity: shares, additional paid-in capital, retained earnings and own shares.

The exact set of items included in a balance sheet will depend on the types of commercial transactions in which an organization is involved. Generally, the items used for the balance sheets of companies located in the same industry will be similar, as they all deal with the same types of transactions. Items are presented in their order of liquidity, which means that the assets that are most readily convertible into cash are listed first, and liabilities that must be settled as soon as possible are listed first.

The total amount of assets listed in the balance sheet should always equal the total of all liabilities and equity accounts listed in the balance sheet (also known as the accounting equation), for which the equation is:

Assets = Liabilities + Equity

If this is not the case, a balance sheet is considered to be unbalanced and should not be issued until the underlying accounting error causing the imbalance has been identified and corrected.

3. Cash flow statement

A cash flow statement is one of the financial statements issued by an enterprise and describes the cash flows within and outside the organization. Their particular focus is on the types of activities that create and use cash, which are operations, investments and financing. Although the cash flow statement is generally considered less critical than the income statement and balance sheet, it can be used to discern trends in business performance that are not readily apparent in the rest of the financial statements. It is especially useful when there is a discrepancy between the amount of reported earnings and the amount of net cash flow generated by transactions.

There may be significant differences between the results shown in the income statement and the cash flows in this statement for the following reasons:

- ❖ There are temporary differences between recording a transaction and when the related cash is spent or received.

- ❖ Management may be using aggressive revenue recognition to report revenue for which cash receipts are still in the future.

❖ The business can be asset-intensive and therefore requires large capital investments that do not appear in the income statement, except with a delay such as depreciation.

Many investors feel that the cash flow statement is the most transparent of the financial statements (i.e., the most difficult to avoid), so they tend to rely on it more than on other financial statements to discern the true performance of a business. They can use it to determine the sources and uses of cash.

The cash flows in the statement of account are divided into 3 groups:

❖ *Operating activities:* These are a classification of cash flows within the statement of cash flows. Items classified within this area are the main revenue-generating activity of an entity, so cash flows are generally associated with income and expenses. Examples of cash inflows from operational activities are:

✓ Cash receipts for the sale of goods and services.

✓ Cash receipts from the accounts receivable collection.

✓ Demand settlement cash receipts.

- ✓ Cash receipts from the settlement of insurance claims.

- ✓ Provider reimbursement cash receipts.

- ✓ Cash receipts from licensees.

- ✓

Examples of cash outflows for operating activities are:

- ✓ Cash payments to employees.

- ✓ Cash payments to suppliers.

- ✓ Payment of fines in cash.

- ✓ Cash payments to settle claims.

- ✓ Payment of taxes in cash.

- ✓ Cash refunds to customers.

- ✓ Cash payments to settle asset retirement obligations.

- ✓ Cash payments of interest to creditors.

- ✓ Cash payments of contributions.

The other two classifications used in the cash flow statement are investing and financing activities. The classification of operating activities is the predetermined classification, so if a cash flow does not belong to any of the other classifications, it is placed in operating activities.

- *Investment activities.* Cash flows from investing activities are an item in the statement of cash flows, which is one of the documents comprising the financial statements of an enterprise. This order line contains the sum total of the changes a company experienced during a designated reporting period in investment gain or loss, as well as any new investment or sale of fixed assets. Elements that can be included in the line of investment activities include the following:

  - ✓ Purchase of fixed assets (negative cash flow).

  - ✓ Sale of fixed assets (positive cash flow).

  - ✓ Purchase of investment instruments, such as stocks and bonds (negative cash flow).

  - ✓ Sale of investment instruments, such as stocks and bonds (positive cash flow).

  - ✓ Loan of money (negative cash flow).

  - ✓ Loan collection (positive cash flow).

✓ Product of insurance settlements related to damaged fixed assets (positive cash flow).

If a company reports consolidated financial statements, the above items will aggregate the investment activities of all subsidiaries included in consolidated results.

The cash flow line element of investing activities is one of the most important in the statement of cash flows because it can be a substantial source or use of cash that significantly offsets any positive or negative amount of cash flow generated by operations. It is particularly important in capital-intensive industries, such as manufacturing, which require large investments in fixed assets. When a company reports persistently negative net cash flows for the purchase of fixed assets, this is a strong indicator that the company is in growth mode and believes it can generate a positive return on additional investment.

❖ *Financing activities.* These are activities that will alter a company's capital or loans. Examples of this are: the sale of shares of the company, the repurchase of shares and the payment of dividends.

There are two ways to present a cash flow statement: direct and indirect. The direct method requires an organization to present cash flow information that is directly associated with the elements that trigger cash flows, such as:

- ✓ Cash collected from customers.
- ✓ Interest and dividends received.
- ✓ Cash paid to employees.
- ✓ Cash paid to suppliers.
- ✓ Interested payment.
- ✓ Income taxes paid.

Few organizations collect information as needed for the direct method, so they use the indirect method. Under the indirect approach, the statement begins with the net income or loss reported in the company's income statement, and then makes a series of adjustments to this figure to arrive at the amount of net cash provided by operating activities. These settings generally include the following:

- ✓ Depreciation and amortization.
- ✓ Provision for losses on accounts receivable.
- ✓ Gain or loss on sale of assets.
- ✓ Change in accounts receivable.
- ✓ Inventory change.
- ✓ Change in accounts payable.

The cash flow line element of financing activities is one of the most important elements in the statement of cash flows, as it can represent a substantial source or use of cash that significantly offsets any positive or negative amount of cash flow generated by operations. On the other hand, a smaller organization that has no debts and does not pay dividends may find that it has no financial activities in a reporting period, so it does not need to include this item in its cash flow statement.

It should delve into the reasons for a large positive or negative balance in cash flows from financial activities, as it may, for example, denote the need for a large loan to support ongoing negative cash flows from operations. Therefore, large quantities in this order line can be considered as a trigger for further investigation.

4. Statement of retained earnings

The retained earnings statement reconciles changes in the retained earnings account during a reporting period. The statement begins with the opening balance in the retained earnings account and then adds or subtracts items such as earnings and dividend payments to arrive at the ending balance of retained earnings. The general calculation structure of the declaration is:

Initial Retained Earnings + Net Income - Dividends = Final Retained Earnings

The retained earnings statement is most commonly presented as a separate statement but can also be added at the end of another financial statement.

Example of the declaration of retained earnings

The following example shows the most simplified version of a retained earnings statement:

Arnold Construction Company

Statement of retained earnings

for the year ended 12 / 31x2

Retained earnings at December 31, 20x1	$150,000
Net income at the year ended December 31, 20X2	40,000
Dividends paid to shareholders	-25,000
Retained earnings at December 31, 20X2	$165,000

The statement is most commonly used when financial statements are issued to entities outside of a business, such as investors and lenders. When financial statements are developed strictly for internal use, this statement is generally not included, because it is not necessary from an operational perspective.

When financial statements are issued internally, the management team generally sees only the income statement and balance sheet, as these documents are relatively easy to prepare.

The four basic financial principles may be accompanied by extensive disclosures that provide additional information on certain topics, as defined by the relevant accounting framework (such as generally accepted accounting principles).

Chapter 5: Benefits of Financial Statements

There are many benefits of financial information, so a company should want to maintain detailed and accurate financial statements. On one hand, there are financial reporting requirements if your company is a public company with investors and shareholders. On the other hand, if you pay taxes to the Internal Revenue Service, you will have to share a lot of information about your income, expenses, debts and other information about your assets and liabilities.

Some research suggests that by analyzing financial statement data, management can make more informed decisions about how the organization works and increase marketing productivity by up to 20%. Based on the fact that companies around the world spend a total of approximately $1 trillion each year on marketing, that can add up to approximately $200 billion. Increasing productivity is undoubtedly one of the many advantages of financial statements that make it worth paying attention to the information provided in them.

In addition to the legal ramifications of not maintaining good books, there are many other benefits of the financial information that financial statements provide to the long-term health and growth of a business. Each has its own role to play in the snapshot it offers.

Better debt management. The amount of debt your business has and how it is owed is an important measure of the financial health of your business. Financial statements separate your assets from liabilities and give you an idea of what you owe compared to what you're contributing.

One of the advantages of financial statements is knowing what your liquid assets are so you can help manage the debts you have and pay off higher-cost liabilities first.

Identifying trends. Financial statements help a company's management to quickly and thoroughly analyze the ways in which they have been doing business over a period of time, as well as to identify any past or present trends that may lead to future problems that need to be addressed immediately. They can also be used to identify sales and growth trends that could lead to higher profitability.

Real-time progress tracking. Financial statements are designed to be fluid documents that change many times over the course of a reporting period, depending on many different income and expense factors. Therefore, paying close attention to statements such as the balance sheet can make it easier to make important decisions as things happen, rather than having to respond retroactively to receiving bad news later.

Passive management. Every business has liabilities ranging from commercial loans to credit cards, supplier accounts and other accounts payable. It is always a good idea to have this information available, and if you apply for most loans or lines of credit, you are generally expected to have this information available quickly and in an easy-to-read format.

Progress and compliance. Another of the many advantages of financial statements is that, by having a series of accurate financial documents, it will be much easier for you to evaluate whether your business is progressing or not.

In addition, if the company is ever audited, the first thing an accountant will request is the company's financial statements in order to comply with generally accepted auditing standards governing its industry.

In addition, they are subject to the financial reporting requirements required by law to report if their documents do not meet the standards. That can look bad for government regulators and investors.

Advantages and disadvantages of financial statements

Advantage: the ability to detect patterns

Financial statements reveal how much a company earns per year in sales. Sales may fluctuate, but financial planners must be able to identify a pattern over years of sales figures. For example, the company may have a pattern of higher sales when a new product is launched. Sales may fall after about a year of being in the market. This is beneficial, as it shows potential and sales patterns so that executives know they expect a drop in sales.

Advantage: a possibility of budgeting

Another advantage of using financial statements for future planning and decision making is that they show the company's budgets. Budgets reveal how much room for maneuver the company has to launch products, develop marketing campaigns or expand the current size of the office. Knowing how much money is available for planning and decision making ensures that the company does not spend more than expected.

Disadvantage: based on market patterns

One disadvantage of using financial statements for decision making is that the facts and figures are market-based at the time. Depending on the market, it can change quickly, so executives should not assume that the numbers in a previous financial statement will remain the same or increase. The fact that a company has sold 5 million copies of a product in one year does not guarantee that it will sell the same quantity or more. You can sell a lot less if a competitor launches a similar product.

Disadvantage: one analysis at a time

Another disadvantage is that a single financial statement only shows how a company is doing at that time. The financial statement does not show whether the company is better or worse than the previous year, for example. If executives decide to use financial statements to make decisions about the future, they should use several financial statements from previous months and years to make sure they have a general idea of how much the company is doing. The financial statement becomes a continuous analysis, which is more useful than using a single statement.

6 Steps to Effective Analysis of Financial Statements

For any financial professional, it is important to know how to effectively analyze a company's financial statements. This requires an understanding of three key areas:

- ✓ The structure of the financial statements.

- ✓ The economic characteristics of the industry in which the company operates.

- ✓ The strategies that the company pursues to differentiate itself from its competitors.

There are generally six steps to developing an effective analysis of financial statements.

1. Identify the economic characteristics of the industry.

First, determine a value chain analysis for industry: the chain of activities involved in the creation, manufacture and distribution of the company's products and/or services. Techniques such as Porter's five forces or the analysis of economic attributes are generally used in this step.

2. Identify company strategies.

Next, look at the nature of the product/service the company offers, including the uniqueness of the product, the level of profit margins, building brand loyalty, and controlling costs. In addition, factors such as supply chain integration, geographical diversification and industry diversification should be considered.

3. Evaluate the quality of the company's financial statements.

Review key financial statements within the context of the relevant accounting standards. When examining balance sheet accounts, issues such as recognition, valuation and classification are key to proper evaluation. The main question should be whether this balance sheet is a complete representation of the economic position of the enterprise. When evaluating the income statement, the main point is to properly evaluate the quality of the earnings as a complete representation of the company's economic performance. Assessing the cash flow statement helps to understand the impact of the company's liquidity position on its operations, investments and financial activities during the period, in essence, where the funds come from, where they go and how the company's overall liquidity was.

4. Analyze current risk and profitability

This is the step where financial professionals can really add value in evaluating the company and its financial statements. The most common analysis tools are the key relationships of financial statements related to liquidity, asset management, profitability, debt management/coverage and risk/market valuation. With regard to profitability, there are two general questions to be asked: How profitable are the company's operations in relation to its assets? regardless of how the company finances those assets, and how profitable is the company from a shareholder perspective? It is also important to learn how to break down return measures into primary impact factors. Finally, it is fundamental to analyze any financial statement index in a comparative manner, observing the current indexes in relation to those of previous periods or in relation to other companies or industry averages.

5. Prepare planned financial statements.

Although often challenging, financial professionals must make reasonable assumptions about the future of the company (and its industry) and determine how these assumptions will affect both cash flows and financing. This often takes the form of pro forma financial statements, based on techniques such as the percentage of sales approach.

6. Value the company.

While there are many valuation approaches, the most common is a type of discounted cash flow methodology. These cash flows could be in the form of projected dividends, or more detailed techniques, such as free cash flows for equity holders or on an enterprise basis. Other approaches may include the use of relative valuation or measures based on accounting, such as economic value added.

Bibliographic References

Bodoo, S. (2014). The road to financial freedom. Retrieved from https://books.google.com.pe/books?id=Sz2lAwAAQBAJrintsec=frontcoverq=libertad+financiera&hl=en&sa=X&ved=0ahUKEwiYsrmFs4vlAhUEvFkKHb-KDAAQ6AEIKzAA#v=onepage&q=libertad%20financiera&f=false

Deambrogio, V. (2004). Basic Guide to Financial Freedom. Retrieved from https://books.google.com.pe/books?id=ICJG4n6h128Cg=PA3q=libertad+financiera&hl=en&sa=X&ved=0ahUKEwiYsrmFs4vlAhUEvFkKHb-KDAAQ6AEIUjAF#v=onepage&q=libertad%20financiera&f=false

Robin,V. y Dominguez, J. (1992). Your Money or Your Life, Viking. Your Money or Your Life. Recuperado de https://yourmoneyoryourlife.com/book-summary/

Fisker,J (2010) Early Retirement Extreme: A philosophical and practical guide to financial independence.   Recuperado   de https://epdf.pub/early-retirement-extreme-a-philosophical-and-practical-guide-to-financial-indepe.html

Cummuta, J.(2002) "The Myths & Realities of Achieving Financial Independence". Recuperado de https://www.nightingale.com/articles/the-myths-realities-of-achieving-financial-independence/

Bryant, B. (2018). The advantages and disadvantages of financial statement analysis. Retrieved from https://www.cuidatudinero.com/13182105/las-ventajas-y-desventajas-de-los-analisis-de-estados-financieros

Concha, P. (2004). Evaluation of financial statements. Retrieved from https://books.google.com.pe/books?id=8LR1 BznKRjICg=PA30q=principios+from+financi al+states&hl=en&sa=X&ved=0ahUKEwj_jdP gsovlAhUNjlkKHeiSBGAQ6AEIOzAC#v=on epage&q=principles%20of%20of%20states%20 financial&f=false

How to Stop Living Paycheck to Paycheck: Volume 3

How to take control of your money and your financial freedom starting today

By

Income Mastery

CHAPTER 1: ONLINE OPPORTUNITIES

Every day technology continues to advance along with the opportunities to make money in a non-traditional way. thanks to the advancement of the internet, people can obtain information easily, they can communicate anywhere in the world without language barriers and they can work from anywhere in the world. Internet has also created a totally new field for people who want to become entrepreneurs and create their own businesses using the Internet. Anyone who has knowledge about the Internet and how to use it, can take advantage of this and can make a fortune with effort and dedication.

Thanks to this book you will have the opportunity to learn how to generate income. Most people have knowledge of a specific topic because they work on it or have studied it. By sharing this knowledge, you can generate an extra income. If you are dubious about teaching a certain topic, you can choose one which passion you, like for example talking about your experience in a restaurant or the trip you made to the beach. You can share anything, but you always have to keep in mind that the idea is for you to sell whatever you are talking about. You need to sell the experience and information. This is just one of several ways to generate income through the internet. In the following book, we will explain how to stop living paycheck to paycheck by increasing your income using the Internet.

CHAPTER 2: Learn about the stock market

To begin with, we must first understand what financial freedom is and what it means to you. We could say that financial freedom is when a person has the freedom to do what they like without having to worry about paying debts, rent, utilities or anything else, that means, using their time however they prefer without worries.

Currently there are a lot of online investment systems that allow us to have many options, each of them allows us really good possibilities when making our investment and that is why we must learn how to invest in the Internet.

We must understand what the stock market is and the different types of investment. The stock market can become a very good source of income if you know how to invest, this may be the gold mine that you are looking for and will help you with your current financial situation, but you must understand that investing is a bet and it is not always easy, sometimes you win and sometimes you lose. This is why it is important to understand the factors which affect the market.

107

The stock exchange is a place where different types of shares, businesses, bonds and other assets are traded. The idea is to buy and sell shares to generate income. With the growth of the internet it was just a matter of time before you could invest in the stock market virtually, without having to go to the bank.

You can invest from home with a computer or through a cell phone locating different online platforms, brokers and intermediary agencies that offer their services to trade your money.

How does the stock exchange work?

It is usually a place where many companies sell part of their shares where you can buy stocks and thus become a shareholder, which means that you now own a small "part" of this company. If the company's profits go up, so does the price of its shares and so does your money, then you will be making money this way, but if the profits go down, so does the price of its shares and so does the price of your shares, in other words, you are losing money if it goes down more than the price at which you bought. This is a very basic form of what the stock exchange is, you have to understand that there you can trade in stocks, binary options, bonds, funds and even in crypto currencies.

Investing in the stock market online has the same basic principles of ownership and investment in shares, however, it differs in how is done. On the online exchange, transactions must be carried out through intermediaries who are in charge of carrying out the exchanges on your behalf. The important thing about this is that you can make these transactions from anywhere via the internet.

Now that you know about the stock market, how it works and how to invest online you need to understand "the online broker", because this will be your great tool to agree to invest no matter where you are or what method you use (computer or cell phone).

Where to invest?

There are many products in which we can invest but the best way to do so is to first acknowledge the various risks of our investments. An important point when deciding to invest is to consider diversification, i.e. not to put all our money into one investment but to seek to have different types of investment in different markets.

People who decide to invest in the stock market do so through brokers. These are entities that allow us to invest in the market through the internet with them, both in the national and international markets, in any company that is listed in the world whether large, medium or small, there are many websites, banks and brokers that allow you to do it from the comfort of your home. Choosing a broker who has access to international markets is a good option because it will allow us to diversify our options.

What expenses can I have when investing?

It is important to know about the expenses that can be presented at the time of investing since this can harm you at the time of obtaining a greater stability in your investment. Because when it comes to investing with brokers, they can have a high rate of commissions.

Purchase and sale commission: This is the main commission we face when investing and applies when we buy financial stocks and when we sell the product. Online brokers usually offer services with low commissions, an example of which is the Degiro broker.

Custody Fee: A fee charged by brokers for holding securities in the account. Some no longer charge for this type of service depending on the number of operations.

 Recommendations to look for a good broker

Make sure you choose a broker who is regulated by law, to guarantee his legitimacy.

Access a multitude of products and markets by choosing a broker that has a variety of products which will allow you to diversify your investments efficiently and reduce the risks of your portfolio.

It is important to work with low operating commissions, so it is important to understand the operating costs of the brokers you choose and verify that you have no hidden costs to avoid surprises.

Degiro, 'Best broker for 2018 shares'.

Dutch broker Degiro was chosen for the third consecutive year as 'Best Broker for 2018 Shares' by the Rankia financial community.

The most popular pages in the investment world are "Plus500" and "eToro" but later I'll tell you about the sites you should check to see what you like the most.

About plus500

In 2008 the company Plus500 was founded with the launch of its online PC platform. This is a provider of contracts, which offers conditions for trading shares, Forex, commodities, crypto currencies, etc. thanks to advances in technology it is possible this form of trading, which allows you to make negotiations in a safe way for small investors from anywhere in the world.

This company is located in the United Kingdom, in the city of London and is supervised by the Financial

Conduct Authority (FCA) of the United Kingdom. The company offers a portfolio of more than 1,000 instruments to all of its clients, making it the fastest growing CFD provider in Europe and Asia.

About eToro.

Since 2007, the eToro platform has been launched changing the traditional investment world and giving everyone access to Internet traces. It is a multi-asset brokerage company that allows social trading. It has registered offices in Cyprus, Israel, China and the United Kingdom. Similarly, it has an investment platform that offers a manual and automatic feature by allowing you to follow other investors and make the same investments they make, this is due to its Copy Trader section, which copies in real time what the investor you follow is doing.

For manual investors, eToro offers a range of professional tools and analysis, providing you with information on stock selection, currencies, commodities, crypto currencies, etc...

About XTB Opinions

This is a broker specialized in the financial products market. It was created in 2002 and has grown to become one of the leaders in online trading offering more than 1500 different markets.

As one of the most popular brokers, it has expanded significantly and has become the leader in the Spanish-speaking market by developing activities in more than 14 countries in Europe, Asia and Latin America. This broker is regulated by FCA and CNMV, offers the best investment school in Latin America, has the best trading platforms including xStation5 and Met trader.

About darwinex.

This is a broker that focuses on the Forex and CFD market. It has a system of segregated accounts which serves to protect its clients' funds, so when it comes to guarantee and security, it has them all.

Darwinex calls trading strategies "darwins". You can create your own darwins and charge commissions when your darwins are copied for profit.

About Avatrade

This is one of the online Forex and Contracts for Difference (CFD) brokers that is growing rapidly in 2019, this is due to the wide variety of assets it offers to invest and on the other hand because this platform is regulated by the Central Bank of Ireland, unlike most CFD brokers that are regulated by CySEC. One of the advantages of using this platform is the amount of options you have to invest either in the Forex market, commodities, stocks or crypto currencies. And also, because it has several forms of copy trading that include:

Robox: a robotic system which allows you to work in Forex.

Mirror trading: it is an item of automatic copy of the traders and operators that we want.

Zulutrade: one of the Copytrading classics which we can connect directly to our avatrade account.

About IQ Option

This is the leading online binary options broker, with more than 20 million satisfied customers trading on its platform every day. This is regulated by CySEC which offers full guarantees of reliability.

One of the advantages of using IQ option is that it has a detailed trading platform that was developed by its engineers and that you can open an account with as little as 10 euros and that allows unit trades from 1 euro.

About PEPPERSTONE

This is an online trading platform that specializes in Forex and Forex trading through Contracts for Difference (CFD). It was created in 2010 and is characterized by its very low service commissions. It is regulated by the FCA (United Kingdom Regulatory Entity). Thanks to the wide arsenal of this broker including Metatrader 4 and Metatrader 5 and specific applications for Android, tablets and iPhone, no operation will be out of your reach.

Cyprus Securities and Exchange Commission CySEC is the highest financial authority of Cyprus, which is responsible for regulating financial markets and ensuring their security and transparency.

CHAPTER 3: Learn how to manage your money.

To begin our journey to financial freedom with the opportunities presented to us online. First we will have to begin to manage our money, this will be a difficult decision because in order to achieve the objective we set ourselves, we have to change our way of thinking and being, we have to know how much money we are earning in our work and how much we are losing in daily expenses. We have to make a record of our expenses: car, house, telephone, television and others. The first thing we should do is stop using our credit cards, stop acquiring debt and start living to the fullest. An example of this is that if we decide to buy a television and the price of this one on credit is worth 30% more than the price of the same equipment in debit but it allows you to pay it little by little, this is a debt that makes your monthly money more difficult for you to save it, because you will always be charged monthly for a certain time and the interest charged by banks on credit cards continue to grow. That's why you have to focus on reducing your expenses, you have to start saving your money. Offer to save 10% of your monthly income, create a bank account and if you can configure this account to give you a discount of 10% of your monthly money, so you will stop seeing that money that is not in your account, if not that this money goes directly to your other savings account.

You have to learn to say NO when you need to buy something, and you don't have the money in your account but remember that you have money saved and you could use it to buy what you want. You have to think that you are collecting money to get your financial freedom and if you start touching that money you have been saving for some time, you will not be able to leave the place where you are, so you must say NO. When you are invited to a bar or a record, think about how that will help you change your economic situation, if it presents a contribution to the change happens you can access but if the answer is negative, you have to say NO. you have to change the way you are living and if it is necessary to change the people around you, do it, you have to know people who think about a better future, who think about making money and not only think about it, but who are always looking for the way forward, looking for information about the market, thinking about how to change the economic situation or as the millionaires would say: You have to surround yourself with master minds. This will help you understand that changing your attitude is easier to learn how to save money and where to spend it.

After this we will begin to invest in ourselves. You have to decide what you want, how much money you need to live as you want, what you have to learn and how to learn, how much time you have to use to achieve what you want. You have to create an image of yourself in the future, how you would like things to be. You have to start taking care of yourself through preparation. Before starting to invest, we have to organize our lives, our expenses and our income in order to move towards the right direction, to achieve the goals we have set for ourselves.

In summary, to manage your money you can follow this series of steps:

1.- Record your expenses. This is the first step to saving your money, you need to know how much you are spending for a month.

Make a budget: After recording your monthly expenses, you can organize a budget of what you can spend monthly and what you can save.

3.- Plan your money saving: Taking into account monthly expenses and income, create a savings portfolio where you have to deliver a minimum of 10% of your monthly income.

Establish objectives: Taking into account your monthly income, propose quarterly or half-yearly objectives which give you an idea of how much you have to save to reach those objectives.

5.- Have priorities: Each person has priorities, according to this is that they decide to save money, find your priorities and focus your savings plans on it.

6.- Save money with automatic transfers: Choose how often you want to transfer money from your primary account to your savings account.

7.- Watch your savings grow: Monitor the progress of your monthly savings, this will help you improve the ways you can achieve your goals.

Here's a passage that I liked a lot and I think is the basis for everyone who wants to start creating their wealth.

"Wealth, like a tree, is born of a seed. The first coin you save will be the seed of the tree that will make your wealth grow."

The richest man in Babylon, GEORGE S CLASON

CHAPTER 4: Learn how to manage your time.

Part of the whole world of online investment depends on the information you manage, that's why you must learn to manage the time you have to look for information about the stock market and the different companies that are in this place.

You have to know how to schedule your free time, you have a family and you want to spend time with them, but you also worry about the expenses you have to give them and the life they want. That's why we have to find a space to learn about the different ways in which you can earn extra money from home, because the more information you have, it will be easier to know where you can invest your money and your time to achieve what many already have, financial freedom.

The time you have to learn will give you the necessary tools to know everything about the different instruments that exist to create wealth. Some tips that might help you get started may be:

Don't spend your time on things you can't control, concentrate on the things you can do and how to do them to get what you need, always think if what you're about to do is going to give you something you're looking for, if the answer is no, then change and find another way.

Do not expect results immediately, this is always a problem because many of those who start in this, want to be rewarded for their effort immediately, when the truth is that this is a world where profits are reflected as time goes by, everything starts slow and grows slowly. So, don't despair and be patient, things will come in their time, just keep focused on what you want to achieve.

Don't give up for failing the first time, no one has ever succeeded in their first attempt. You always have to keep trying and at some point you will, that's why patience and time are important factors in creating income.

Don't let others influence your emotions and discourage you by seeing that you can't earn extra income, remember that you're the one who's trying without giving up because you know it's just a matter of time before you get what you're looking for. Remember that you are trying while those people who want to influence you to quit don't even have the courage to try for fear of failure. Go ahead and don't let anyone discourage you.

Here are some tips you can implement to help you make the most of your time:

1. Leave aside perfectionism and seek to produce good results.

2. Organize your activities. Keep in mind the tasks you have to do each day and organize everything so you can make the most of your time.

3. Perform a cleaning: Change the work area where you develop, clean everything both physically and mentally and you will be able to focus better your goals.

Find out what skills and abilities you possess so that you can develop better and focus your energy on that.

CHAPTER 5: POLLING PAGES.

Paid surveys have become one of the methods most used to generate income through the Internet, since to access it you only need to have time and access to the Internet.

Large companies have always looked for ways to get information about what consumers think of their products, that's why they use the survey method, which allows you to use methods of research and data collection that are then used to get a report of what people think about various issues, these have a variety of purposes and are carried out in many ways, that's why companies ask promotions and consumer questions.

Today there are an infinite number of websites that offer services to companies to obtain information through surveys and reach customers directly so that they can give their opinion on what they think of their products. These polling pages are responsible for placing these orders via the Internet and in turn give some financial compensation to people who devote their time to solve the tests on a product. All of this varies according to the company requesting the market study and the amount of time they have available to carry out the study.

Due to the growing need for extra money, people from all over the world have decided to take this as a way to generate income, turning it into a second job, which allows you to earn an extra by conducting such surveys. If you want to start earning money in this way you need to understand that the earnings you get from a single survey will not be very large but with effort and dedication you can get a good weekly amount.

If you have been interested in this way of generating income, it would be good to investigate a little more about the different polling pages that exist in the world and those that can be found for your region. Some of the most popular pages for solving surveys are inbox dollars, swag bugs, toluna, and many others, which allow you to earn dollars directly through their platforms and doing other tasks. Not only are they useful for solving surveys, but they can also ask you to watch some videos, share pages or subscribe to other pages and with that pay you a few cents of dollars. Just like these, there are other sites that pay you to try their products or make promotions.

That's why paid surveys are a completely viable option, thanks to the ease and speed with which you can complete, but even as simple as it may be to do a survey, it is difficult to find offers that are worthwhile, that's why as you gain experience in this field, you can go looking for ways to work on several pages at the same time.

If you've been interested in the world of surveys and want to get into it, here I'll leave you some of the most popular polling pages:

Time bucks.

This platform is more than just solving surveys. In it you can find offers to make money watching videos, slides, install applications and following people in a social network.

LifePoint's

It is one of the best-known platforms in Spain and Latin America, which allows you to win by solving a survey.

Toluna.

This is an online community with more than 10 million members around the world. This pollster pays you a series of points for each one you solve.

ISurveyWorld.

This is a page to earn money with surveys, you can solve surveys of products and services of daily use. This page pays directly in dollars via PayPal, and your surveys are made to last between 10 and 15 minutes.

Surveyeah

It is a survey platform that is available for several Latin American countries. One of its main benefits is that it has a 24-hour technical support which serves to resolve many questions. This platform sends the available survey notifications via the email you provide at the time of registration.

Now that you know some of the pages that you can use if you are interested in online paid surveys, there are many other pages that you can use and every day more spaces are created for this type of work, you only have to devote part of your time to be able to achieve a weekly income that allows you to reach your goals.

CHAPTER 6: Application

Surely when reading this book you have your phone nearby and is that we can no longer live without the cell phone, even children get to have a cell phone at a very early age but the truth is that your phone would not be very useful without the applications that make it work as you like.

And it is that an application is nothing more than a program created to carry out or facilitate a task in a computer device and it is that nowadays the applications can be created by any person and that this can generate millions of dollars when gaining popularity. An example would be the application of the one million dollars "Instagram". This application was created by several people, who wanted to share with their friends the photos of their travels instantly and this way they came up with the idea of creating the application "Instagram" becoming the most famous application of visual content and thanks to this, managed to get millions of downloads, which caught the attention of billionaire Mark Zuckerberg. Creator and founder of the world's largest social network "Facebook" which would buy the rights to the application for more than $1 billion.

As well as this, there are many applications that are launched to the market every day, for all tastes and colors. If you have an idea that could become the next million dollar application, I encourage you to immerse yourself in this world, it is not necessary to know how to program to create your application but you must have some basic knowledge about the subject. On the Internet there are many tutorials on how to create applications and if you do not want to study, you can also hire a programmer or find a friend to join and create the next millionaire application.

A lot can be said about the entrepreneurs who decide to create their application: luck stroke? or talent? the truth is that a few years ago, nobody thought they could become a millionaire by creating a game for mobile.

There are many programs that allow you to create an application from your computer in a very simple way to programs with endless tools that will give you the opportunity to create much more complex applications, you must take into account some of these tips if you want to create an application.

Tips for creating an application.

1. The first thing you should have is an idea or a way to solve a problem. If you still don't have an idea and don't know what to do, think that all the

applications have been created to solve a problem or to make things easier.

2. There is a Google application called Google Keyword Planner which lets you know how many people are looking for what you are trying to do.

3. When you have the idea, it's time to detail the qualities of what you want, you have to capture all the characteristics of this.

4. After detailing the features of your application, you have to do a study to verify which are the most essential and which you can leave to be added through updates.

5. The design you choose for your app is also important, since it determines the way in which the user will use your application.

Once you list the bases of your app it is time to create your application through a development program or you can hire a programmer to do it for you.

Programs you can use

Java SDK.

It is a development software which provides tools for the creation of java programs. This tool can be used from a single computer or from multiple computers connected on the same network and work as a single application.

Microsoft Visual Studio. NET

This is a set of tools and software development technology for creating high performance applications. It allows you to create websites and applications for any platform.

NetBeans

This is a free development environment, created primarily for java development. There are an important number of modules that allow you to expand your functions.

However, if you're not interested in creating applications because you think there are a lot of them already or you don't have an idea about which application to create, then what would you say if there was an application that paid you to use it? Sounds good right? there are many applications which allow you to earn money using their portal, many of these only require you to invite people to download the application and pay you in tokens, coins, diamonds that then you can change to dollars or euros to be sent to your account. In this modality the way to earn money is by attracting people to download your application and pay you a small percentage, the fastest way to use this method is to use your social networks, whether Instagram, Facebook,

WhatsApp or any other that you like, which serves to advertise on the applications you use and thus make you bigger and bigger your group.

These applications don't just pay you to get people to download your App. Many ask you to perform a series of daily tasks which will give you a higher percentage than you get by inviting people but you can also add to the daily earnings and make your income bigger this way.

Many of these applications have time in the market and worldwide recognition, as they remain stable over time and make their payments quickly and accurately. It wouldn't be wrong to check this way of generating income, it's something you can do from your cell phone at any time just by using a few minutes a day. This is a slow but sure way to create income without taking up much of your time and if you add it to the different ways you choose to get something extra, you will be bringing an extra lot to your wallet.

1. Gift Huter Club

This has a website and an application available for Android, which allows you to earn points by doing different tasks such as watching videos, testing apps, solving surveys or with contests, the points you can earn with this, are then changed to money that you can then send to your PayPal account. It also has two levels of referrals, that is, if you invite someone you will win 10% of what that person wins and if your guest invites another person, you will win 5% of what they win.

2. Cash pirate

This is an application similar to the previous one, that is, it pays you to accomplish a series of tasks, downloading applications, watching videos or inviting people to join.

3. Cash app

It is a platform for Android and iOS which allows you to earn money quickly and easily through its platform, which is very entertaining and easy to use.

4. Click and walk

This is an application which pays you to fulfill a series of missions such as taking a picture, watching a video or giving your opinion about a store.

5. Google Opinion Rewards

This is a very popular application which gives you short polls about a place you have visited lately and in return you will receive a payment in the form of play store credits for your opinion.

CHAPTER 7: SOCIAL NETWORKS

In these moments the social networks have had an important denouement in all parts of the world due to how fast the information can arrive from one place of the world to another breaking the barrier of the language and it is for this reason that nowadays infinities of people exist creating profiles in the social networks to share their ideals, thoughts, trips, videos, works, etc... and as it is growing.

The objective of working in social networks is to attract the attention of companies, which access these media to promote any kind of product and thus achieve what we could call a virtual market, which offers a great opportunity for everyone.

If you are interested in social networks such as Facebook, Instagram, Snapchat, etc... You can create a profile or possibly you already have it but now how to use it to create income? Well, you can promote something that you have to offer to the world, be it your knowledge, stories, videos, etc. The truth is that for your social network to become a source of income you have to get the attention of thousands of people who like your publications, this is what is always sought, get thousands and thousands of people to stop to see your page and then you can start monetizing in various ways that I will tell you now.

You can sell mentions for webmasters, web pages or Pages fans. You only have to mention these people, leaving a link in your publication and start charging for each of the people who visit the pages thanks to every mention you make about them.

Another way is to advertise affiliate products through click bank. With this means you can earn up to 70% of the price of a product, sounds good, right?

There is another way called CPA (cost per action) which pays you for each conversion made by the people who follow your page, an example would be to leave a custom link that directs you to a game. The person who clicks on the link will have to enter some information (email or phone number) and this way you will generate income thanks to your followers.

Quite an interesting way to create revenue through social networking, it's a great way to create a source of revenue if you know how to use it.

I'll give you a series of tips that you can use in your social network to get the attention of customers.

Be ingenious

This is the most basic part if you want to sell something online, especially on Facebook. You have to get users' attention one way or another. To be able to sell you have to pique the curiosity of users making them want to at least click your publication, with this you will get a breakthrough in getting them to see the products you're publishing. Advertising plays a very important role here.

Use videos.

The best way to show users a product is through a video. Users will quickly understand what it's all about and will be able to decide whether or not they want the product with just a few seconds of your video.

Create expectation

Here you can talk about the benefits that can have some of your products or the products you advertise so that your potential customers can know these benefits. The purpose of this is that your potential customer imagines himself using the product and can make a purchase.

Creates offers.

There is the possibility of improving your sales on Facebook if you create promotions, offers or gifts for your customers, this will attract the attention of people about a product and apart win a prize or take advantage of an offer. You can do this on key days such as Valentine's Day, Mother's Day, Father's Day, national holidays and others. This is a great contribution as the customer is tempted by the extra benefit.

Create albums as a catalog.

You can upload photos of various products that you are promoting in the form of a catalog so that your potential customers, to see a photo, have the opportunity to see other products. You have to add a description of each product, this will allow him to know more about what he is seeing, remember that the more creative you are you will be able to get many more profits.

CHAPTER 8: YOUTUBE.

You probably know this page or application. YouTube is the world's largest and best-known video site. Daily videos are being created to be published and shown to the world. From movie videos to tutorials, online classes, courses, animations and many other types of videos but do you know why millions of people are encouraged to create their videos and put them on this page? It's because they can generate passive income through videos. As they become famous and people watch them, they gain followers and attract many more people. But this is something that is achieved with a lot of time and dedication.

The way to generate revenue through YouTube is to place ads in your videos which will pay a percentage for each ad that subscribers see, in a video you can place amounts of ads but remember that this can get to upset followers and let them continue watching your videos.

If you have been interested in this way of generating income through videos, I will explain how to start in this world of YouTuber and here are a few steps you can follow if you want to try.

1. Create your channel. This will be your presence in the world of YouTube and at the same time it

will be the same account you use for Google. When you create your YouTube account, you'll also create an account on Gmail and Google Drive. To make your channel a little easier to find, you can add keywords related to the videos you are thinking of uploading to your channel.

2. Add content to your channel. You have to upload high quality videos to your channel to attract more subscribers. Your videos may not be very good at first but remember that practice makes perfect. Uploading videos regularly will make your followers more captive to your next post, so be sure to add a striking description of your post.

3. The key to monetizing your channel is that your audience watches the ads you put in your videos. For this it is good to keep earning more subscribers. You must always improve the quality of your videos and so will increase the number of people who will follow your channel. You can also interact with your followers, answering their questions, sending them greetings or whatever else you do so they feel you are taking them into account.

4. Start monetizing your account. Click on the option to monetize your channel and you will see a weight symbol "$" next to the videos you

already have on your page, this will make from now on YouTube is responsible for advertising in the videos you select.

5. Use social networks. You can create a blog or use your social networks to publish your videos and be able to reach many more people than although they enter YouTube, do not seek your videos thanks to the large number of videos that exist. So why not look for ways to get your videos to more people without them having to search for them themselves? In this way you make sure to reach more people and go looking for more public which will take care that you start earning money.

If you have decided to become a YouTuber and use this medium to generate your income, then you must keep in mind that the more specific your channel is, the more chances you have that it will begin to grow rapidly and that your audience will increase exponentially, for this you must take into account the following things:

o   Gender: It's important to know where your videos are headed.

o   Age: To know in what rank are the majority of users who can become your followers.

o <u>Geographical location</u>: It is important to determine in which countries or cities the largest number of your users are collected.

CHAPTER 9: FREELANCER

A FreeLancer is a person who "has no boss", is his own boss, owns his own company and offers his services to third parties in exchange for a financial remuneration. Bearing this in mind, you have to know that entering the world of FreeLancer does not guarantee you a passive monthly income, it does not work this way. To earn money in this way you have to offer your services according to your knowledge.

Many people who start working this way do so because of the constant changes we have in our daily lives and in this way they can work from home without having to leave their workplace where they do not feel comfortable, where they have long hours of travel to get there on time, where a person is demanding more and more every day.

That's why many people choose to become FreeLancer, whatever their motivation, the main thing is to manage their own work time, you decide how many hours a day you need to work to achieve the goal you have set or the work you have been asked to do, you have to know that the earnings you get through this way of working, will depend on the amount of work you get by offering your services online.

There is a market for FreeLancer requested daily and they have greater demand. One of the pages for this type of work is "Workana". This page publishes a study called "Independent Work Report and Entrepreneurship" with the intention of discovering the market situation and measuring the growth of FreeLancer work.

The categories that most often stand out in this field are those related to the Internet, whether digital marketing and programming or web development. But this is only a study that determines which are the categories that most often have demand for work, the truth is that anyone can become a FreeLancer worker, what is needed for this is to have responsibility and skills that can serve to perform any type of activity, as there are infinite tasks that can be done as: programmer, graphic designer, translator, editor, salesman, photographer, teacher, event organizer and many more. In many cases it doesn't matter if you don't have higher education, the important thing is to be able to make known the skills you possess.

Self-employed people have the freedom to manage their workload, and they can choose which projects to work on and reject those they don't want to work on. No one forces them to do work for customers they don't like.

There is no income limit. One of the greatest advantages of being a FreeLancer is that you can generate a considerable amount of income when you already have a career with experience in this field, making you a fixed clientele, which will turn to you to assign some tasks. From the beginning working as a FreeLancer is difficult but when you get a portfolio of potential customers you can get to have a really large income considering what a person generates in a regular job.

If you have decided that this is your option, that you have something to offer and you can get a portfolio of clients on the Internet, you must bear in mind that you must select an area in which you can develop effectively and be able to give the most of yourself to start working independently.

After deciding what service you want to offer, you have to create a portfolio which will be your image before the clients so that they have a good reference about your abilities and the way in which you can carry out the tasks, this way you will be attracting the attention of your potential clients.

One of the common mistakes made by people who start working independently is to offer a very low price for their services. It is known that the pressure that is received for not obtaining income is great and not for that reason you must put a price below the price of the market, that will not speak very well of you, the best thing is that you speak a price with your client which is reasonable. Same job, same pay.

About Nubelo

This is a FreeLancer work platform which has mobile application for Android and iPhone, in it you can find more than 92,000 jobs in areas such as web and mobile development, digital marketing, graphic design, translation, accounting and others.

This service specializes in work that can be done in a digital environment. Registering on this page to do work is completely free, however, a basic profile has several limitations. That's why the site offers a premium account which will give you many benefits.

About Info jobs freelancer.

This is one of the best known websites in Spain to work online, which has more than 151,000 registered professionals who use this medium to work in the area of web development, application development, translation, blogging, and more, although the most numerous jobs are those aimed at technical profiles.

Registration on this page is free of charge, however, it will charge you a commission of 8.5% of the total price agreed with the client for the work requested. It's a point to keep in mind when working on this site.

ABOUT GENIUZZ.

Genius is defined as the "platform for buying and selling small services" this website puts FreeLancer professionals who want to offer services with companies that are looking for workers for their projects. The offers presented in this page are of very varied styles, from the classic writing of documents, design or marketing, to more "mundane" things such as help with the declaration of income, travel arrangements and even elements of craftsmanship.

About Workana.

This platform is centered in Latin America and has more than 280,000 FreeLancer registered in it who choose to do work related to the design and development of web pages or applications, video and animations, document writing, translation of texts, marketing campaigns and many more, you can create your profile for free on this website, but you must bear in mind that the page will charge you 20% of what you will charge your client for the work done.

About Fiverr

The operation of this website is a little different to all the previous ones because it does not collect information about the work offered for FreeLancer but are the professionals themselves who are responsible for offering their services in an attractive and as professional as possible to attract the attention of future customers. It is quite peculiar that professionals exhibit many of their work on this page so that people can see the quality of work they can do.

ABOUT GURU.

This site is one of the oldest to offer this type of service, as it was founded in 2001 and today has more than one and a half million users (1,500,000) worldwide and currently has 560,000 job offers, most of these jobs focus on the field of software development, but there are also offers related to art, design, sales, marketing and finance.

In Guru you can open an account for free but this will have certain limitations. To remove these limitations, you have to pay an amount of $9 per month so that you can get rid of the limitations that put on your account, apart from this, Guru charges a small percentage of the total cost for your work.

About Upwork.

This is a page with great potential where you can get a huge number of customers, more than four million (4,000,000). Here you can get job offers related to the creation of applications, design, marketing, customer service, translation, writing, etc. ... As other pages, registration in this is free, but here you will be charged 10% of each payment received for your work, also has the option to create a Premium account which gives you the option to extra features and some benefits.

CHAPTER 10: Amazon

Amazon is one of the largest buying and selling companies in the world, which works around this and its main countries of work are Germany, Austria, France, China, Japan, United States, United Kingdom, Canada, Australia, Italy, Spain, Brazil, Mexico and India. In this way Amazon is able to offer specific products to each region. This company was founded in 1994 by Jeff Bezos after leaving his previous job as vice president of the company "D. E Shaw & Co. That same year.

Amazon began as a bookstore which had a number of titles and that the demand for this article at the time of its founding was too high, which allowed the company to grow exponentially. This bookstore was a total success since in the first two months of life, it managed to reach a total of 45 different countries including the United States. His sales were over $20,000 a week.

This is why Amazon is one of the most varied ways in which we can work, thanks to the fact that it has a number of ways that we will use to generate money. Some of them are not online but it is not superfluous to take into account the information.

Sell articles

Amazon has the particularity of being the largest market in the world, in which you can sell your products and make them reach anyone in any corner of the planet. Now the internationalization of the products is possible thanks to this, of course there are many pages that operate under the same methodology as Amazon, but we focus on this page because it is the best known worldwide.

Browse through their products to get an idea of which are the most in demand or to know which are those that this platform needs.

Amazon Flex - Amazon Deliverer

This is a service offered by the company where people with their own vehicle can work for them by distributing packages for 28 euros a block of two hours. The good thing about this option is that you can choose the schedule that you want to work and you can generate the money that you want because you are going to work the hours that you want.

Works as an Amazon Warehouse

This is a good option to create an income passively, since you can rent a space that you have empty and do not use to make storage for the Amazon company guaranteeing you a money income by renting a space.

The company offers you an option that allows you to make warehouse for products that could not be delivered because of the difficulty it generates to reach the particular buyer. Now think that if you have a space and time, this is an effective way to get some extra income.

I work from home for Amazon

Amazon offers a web service for people to opt to work from home, usually these opportunities grow on holidays, here is where you can find more opportunity to work this way.

The majority of positions that are offered on Amazon in this way are for customer service.

Amazon Affiliate

This is one of the most used modalities nowadays and it is one of the ones that allows you to earn the most money. Today many people work this way. On the internet you can get a lot of blogs that talk about how to work in the Amazon partner system and even on their official website you can get a guide with very useful tips on how to use the Amazon affiliate program and the best thing is that it is totally free.

You can also create a blog where you can recommend Amazon products and use your social networks. The idea of working in this field is to be creative when publishing a product, as Amazon will pay you a commission for each product.

The way to do it is very simple, the first thing you have to do is create an Amazon account, which is completely free.

Then you can choose from the millions of products found in this store and start promoting that product, so you can start earning commissions with the advertising you do to the product and you can get to earn up to 10% of each sale.

A clear example may be that you read a book found in Amazon stores and decide to publish an opinion on this book, then publish that opinion in your blog, social network or YouTube channel. To make it work you have to add your associate link or a link that directs people who visit your blog, to the Amazon store where the book you're talking about is, this way when people make a purchase of the product, automatically you will be earning about 10% of the total cost of the product.

You can do this with any product you find on Amazon, for that there is a wide variety of products.

Publish a book on Amazon.

Amazon gives you the possibility to publish a book of your own edition. By this means you can publish as many books, manga's, recipes, tutorials, etc. ... and start making money passively with the sales you get from your publications.

To achieve this, you don't have to be a great writer, but you have to have basic knowledge and follow a series of steps that Amazon requires when publishing a book.

The publication of a book in Amazon is totally free and can take you a short time to do it, also this one will be available for many people around the world.

Sell handicrafts by Amazon

If you have articles created by yourself you can publish them by Amazon Handmade which is a section of Amazon that allows to publish crafts of own creation, for this you have to send a request to Amazon Handmade which will have to make a check of your product to define that they are original products handmade by you or an employee.

CONCLUSION

In this book, we were able to learn some of the different ways that exist on the Internet to generate income, some passively and others actively. We realized that it all depends on how we want to achieve our goals. Some may take this as a main job and others may choose to work it as an extra, apart from their main job. Aside from the fact that many of these options are tentative you should keep in mind that there is only one thing that all of these methods demand and that is time. Like any company that wants to grow, it all depends on the time and perseverance you devote to building the foundation to grow your source of income.

Remember that this book only served to know the different ways in which you can earn money through this medium.

www.ingramcontent.com/pod-product-compliance
Lightning Source LLC
Chambersburg PA
CBHW050525190326
41458CB00045B/6706/J